THE PHYSICAL COMEDY HANDBOOK

Davis Rider Robinson

HEINEMANN
PORTSMOUTH, NH

Heinemann

361 Hanover Street
Portsmouth, NH 03801–3912
http://www.heinemann.com

Offices and agents throughout the world

Library of Congress Cataloging-in-Publication Data
Robinson, Davis Rider.
    The physical comedy handbook / Davis Rider Robinson.
        p.   cm.
    Includes bibliographical references.
    ISBN 0-325-00114-6
    1. Acting. 2. Comedy—Technique. I. Title.
PN2071.C57R63   1999
792'.028—dc21   99-19681
                                                    CIP

Editor: Lisa A. Barnett
Production: Vicki Kasabian
Cover design: Jenny Jensen Greenleaf
Author photo: Carol Kaplan
Manufacturing: Louise Richardson

Printed in the United States of America on acid-free paper
Sheridan 2018

To Libby Marcus

Contents

Acknowledgments

I would like to thank the many teachers I've come in contact with over the years, in particular Jacques Lecoq, Fay Lecoq, and Norman, Sandra, and Thomas at the Ecole Jacques Lecoq; Tony Montanaro and the rest of the clan at the Celebration Barn Theater; the Berg, Jones, and Sarvis Dance Company; Jonathan Wolken, Mark Morris, Ronlin Foreman, Don Jordan, Bill Irwin, and Avner for their inspiring workshops; my students at Emerson College and Boston University, whose creative energy and willingness to try out new ideas are the basis for many of the exercises in this book; all of the members of Beau Jest Moving Theater—Lisa, Elyse, Larry, Karen, Steve, Lauren, Chris, Tara, Pat, Jay, Mimi, Phil, Bob, Mike, and Alex for their continued inspiration, friendship, and years of dedication to the creation of physical theater; special thanks to Professor Judith Chaffee at Boston University who helped me get started with the planning and execution of this book; Lisa Barnett and Vicki Kasabian for their encouragement and editorial assistance; and to Libby, the love of my life.

Introduction

George Burns once said, "Nowadays, there's no place a kid can go to learn to be lousy." I believe he was referring to the great breeding grounds for comic talent that gave him his start—vaudeville, burlesque, touring theatricals, and theater revues, which have since been replaced by standup comedy clubs, dinner theater, and televised entertainment. Where once there was an active theater in almost every town in America, multiplex cinemas now reign over enormous parking lots. Where once a family of immigrant kids would improve their act by performing four shows a day, six days a week, in towns all over the country, today's aspiring comic performers vie for a chance to be seen on television. The nature of performance has shifted to meet the needs of the small screen, leaving behind a wealth of theatrical vitality gathering dust in boarded up playhouses from Pasaic to Pasadena. Yet the spirit of comedy lives on, as it has through the ages. It pops up on stage, on street corners, in sitcoms, and in movies. The medium has changed, but the message remains the same: Human behavior deserves to be laughed at, and audiences will forever enjoy seeing their foibles revealed. The forces that made sixteenth-century audiences laugh at the Commedia Zanni in the village square are the same universal forces that cause millions to laugh today at the antics of wacky characters on a television sitcom. But where does a performer go these days to learn to be lousy?

This book concerns itself with one aspect of comedy: the spirit of physical play. My interest is practical, not theoretical. There are numerous books and essays that examine comedy from a philosophical, historical, or aesthetic point of view. Few actually provide guidance in how to do it. Comic plays are an important part of every university's season, yet few academic programs offer much in the way of formal comedy training, leaving it up to an actor's intuition. This book provides instruction to actors interested in developing their comic abilities and guidance to teachers structuring that work. Although intuition plays a big part in comic timing, it is also a skill that actors can hone. I disagree with those who say comedy can't be taught. Guided experiments in partner work, timing, focus, obstacles, and space, can give students a clear vocabulary for playing comedy. In countless work-shops I have seen hopelessly unfunny people—with proper guidance and training—do brilliant comic work. They may not end up making it their life's work, but they certainly need not feel out of place in a comedy if they are cast in one.

There is an old saying that understanding comedy is like trying to understand a frog. When you dissect it, you kill the frog. In an effort not to be too formal in structure with an art form that is spontaneous in its execution, this book gives you several ingredients from which to make your own recipes. You may be a director looking for a new bit of business, a teacher interested in helping students improve their scene work, or an actor who wants to be the next Chaplin. Open the book to any page that suits you. Start in the middle or skip to the end. Trial and error has always been my main tool as an actor, director, and teacher, and I urge you to experiment with the ideas in this book as you see fit. This is not a road map for how to write funny material, it is a set of tools for actors to use when playing comedy.

Finding a live audience to be lousy in front of, even a small one, is key to comedy training. Actors in the twenties and thirties had many opportunities to hone their comic skills in sketches performed at parties, in revues, and on Broadway. Street performers learned from their audiences, or they would starve. Whenever possible, create an actor-audience relationship while you are training. The best environment is a class of fourteen to eighteen students, with part of the class serving as audience while others work. If the group is too small, there will be no one to witness group exercises. If it is too big, the pressure to "entertain" is increased and it takes too long to get around to everyone individually. Remember that this nonpaying audience is there to serve the performer, not vice versa. They witness experiments so that actors can see what works. A successful class is guided by a teacher with a good eye who can steer things constructively when someone fails. Groups of twelve, fifteen, and eighteen divide well for trio exercises. In this book, I present exercises as if they were being done in a class of eighteen. I also frequently use the word *improv* as shorthand for improvisation.

One of the keys to comic timing is knowing what you want to communicate to an audience when you are caught in a dilemma. Making clear choices requires lots of practice. It should be understood by your training audience that developmental exercises are not finished sketches. Avoid the temptation of trying to make people laugh. *Trying* to do anything has a tinge of desperation that audiences can detect like the smell of rotting fish. Just do the work. A comic performer trying too hard to be taken seriously is equally painful to watch. Performers, expect no response; audiences, be patient. Trying too hard to get a laugh undermines the comic development of richer themes, short-circuiting any real discoveries that might be made. The atmosphere in class should encourage risk taking and failure. Lots of trial and error eventually leads to positive results.

Once you do have material ready for the public, take it to a real audience. This is when you can see if it will "play in Pasaic." Put on a show, workshop it, or take a paying job and try out your ideas. My first job was for thirty-five dollars, providing entertainment with my juggling partner for a father-son banquet at a local Bonanza Steak House. Do birthday parties, family functions, and civic events. Form your own theater company; try playing the streets. Blue Man Group used to test ideas out on people waiting in lines at theaters, museums, and galleries. If you want more training, there is a list at the back of this book of schools and theater companies that do physical work (see Appendix).

The Comic You

Physical comedy is a noble pursuit with infinite variations. Buster Keaton, Charlie Chaplin, the Marx Brothers, Fannie Brice, Lillian Russell, Laurel and Hardy, Jacques Tati, Lucille Ball, the Honeymooners, Dick Van Dyke, Sid Caesar, Ernie Kovacs, Carol Burnett, Woody Allen, Lily Tomlin, Robin Williams, Steve Martin, and countless others have given the human race something to laugh at. They've come in all shapes and sizes, from elegant to neurotic, stone-faced to in-your-face. Take for instance the simple gag of tripping and losing your composure. Which way is yours? There are many ways to do this act that provoke a laugh and many ways to trip that are not at all funny, particularly if someone gets hurt. A ninety-year-old grandmother falling down would be frightening and great cause for alarm. Yet Barry Lubin, the clown in the Big Apple Circus who plays a character called Grandma, can fall down and we laugh because we know he's not injured, he meant to do it for our pleasure, and he isn't really ninety years old. The context must be right. An actor playing King Lear might get a big laugh by tripping on his first entrance, but it would undermine the credibility of the rest of the play. I humbly hope this book will enhance your physical playfulness while also helping you decide what actions are appropriate for any given context.

Context is only one element in a complex web of moments. There are endless examples of hard-working actors who think the context is right but whose efforts, in my opinion, aren't funny. Just watch television any night. Many of the physical gags you see are predictable, poorly set up, and done with a laugh track. Performers lose touch with the actor-audience relationship. Timing is dictated by a half-hour quota of laughs and commercials. No one pauses for more than ten seconds of silence in a reaction because it's too expensive. Emphasis is on the comedy writer, not the performer. If you watch the actors in *The Honeymooners*, who performed live with the barest of rehearsals, you'll see many refreshing examples of actors thinking and working on their feet. To see a lovely example of timing, find the old video clip of Merv Griffin interviewing Jack Benny. Griffin asked Benny if he remembered his first laugh on stage: Jack waited, and waited, and the longer he waited, the more the audience laughed. Finally he said, "That's the silliest question I ever heard." The lesson in timing is priceless.

MTV, Hollywood, and the information age have accelerated our exposure to images, but I don't think human instincts have changed that much in the past thousand years. Students training for comedy need to turn the clock back a bit. Watch Ernie Kovacs: absurd, without being in a rush. Watch a Preston Sturges screwball comedy to see how masterfully physical gags can be woven into a plot. See how Henry Fonda gets set up for a trip from Barbara Stanwyck in *The Lady Eve*. Rent Jacques Tati films and soak up lessons from a comic genius who really took his time.

Comedy has fared better in the film medium than on television because the two-hour format allows for richer plot and character development. It's also the length of the average stage play. When a film intelligently integrates moments of physical comedy with character and plot, such as *Four Weddings and a Funeral* or *Shakespeare in Love* do, audiences respond enthusiastically. Even a film as intentionally low-brow as *There's Something About Mary* uses strong needs and good context to create some hilarious situations. Chaplin used to spend weeks reshooting the same scene numerous times with small adjustments in order to fine-tune the comic business and the *need* for it to happen. To find good role models for comedy and the human condition, I recommend you avoid television, unless it's *I Love Lucy*, *Dick Van Dyke*, or *The Honeymooners* reruns. Take a look instead at the silent film comedians and the screwball comedy classics of the thirties and forties. They are the mother lode of physical invention.

A troupe of marvelously talented actors-clowns from Russia, the Litsideis, performed in the United States a few years ago. I asked them after their show where they got their training, and they said they had no teacher—watching old Chaplin movies was their only guide. However, observation and admiration is not enough. You must conduct your own experiments. It takes a *lot* of work. Painters start by drawing circles, doing still-lifes. Filmmakers start by making shorts. Actors build comic skills by doing sketches, blackout routines, and lots of improvising. You also get practice every time you try to make a baby or a child laugh. Cheering someone up is a good way of revealing your instincts for physical comedy.

A Philosophy for Falling Down

A grasshopper walks into a bar to get a beer, and the bartender says, "Hey, we've got a drink named after you." "Oh really," says the grasshopper. "A Herbert?!" This is a verbal joke, using linguistic misdirection to conjure up an unlikely scenario in the listener's imagination. Depending on the skill of the teller, laughter may occur. This is also true with physical comedy. It's not the gag, it's the delivery.

In a physical "joke," the grasshopper would walk into the bar (ouch!), turn his head to greet an old friend, and fall over an unseen chair (the Dick Van Dyke method). Again, misdirection and an unexpected event might provoke laughter; it all depends. Comedy is a living thing. What works for one actor might bomb with another. The most carefully choreographed bit of comic business will be futile if the performer is unskilled, if he or she is uncomfortable with the role, or if the situation is forced. Whether working alone or with an ensemble, in scripted, original, or silent scenarios, the degree to which an audience will laugh at any moment is based on several universal principles. Are the performers involved in the moment? Is their dilemma of interest to the audience? Do we care about what happens to them? Are their actions justified according to their character? Do the performers "pay off" what they set you up for with skill, momentum, imagination, joy, and risk? The degree to which you meet all of these conditions will determine whether an audience is engaged in your comic dilemma. I should at this point offer the following disclaimer: *Any rule appearing in this book is meant to be broken.* In comedy, someone is always breaking new ground and proving that every rule has an exception.

No two people have the same chemical makeup, the same set of experiences and memories that create presence on stage. I believe everyone has a comic persona. There are active personalities and reactive personalities, "straight men" and buffoons, tricksters and losers. One of the goals of this book is to help you fine-tune your presence on stage to its greatest comic potential. You may be gentle, you may be aggressive, you may work best as a benign Margaret Dumont (Groucho Marx's foil), or a sputtering Tommy Smothers. Try many things. You may have multiple strengths. You may need a partner, or you may work better solo. You may have a love for Shakespeare, or you may gravitate to the world of Beckett. Is a slow burn more effective for you or a fast double take? Do you like broad expressions, rich language, or silence? Are you an instigator or a receiver? Eventually, your comic persona will surface. Use this information to create life on stage. As a director, I am always leery of blocking a show before seeing how the actors work together. I prefer giving them a variety of options in rehearsal that allow me to see through trial and error where the actors' instincts and the material they interpret truly intersect.

Physical work is essentially a folk art, handed down via oral tradition. It's a bit tricky putting it in written form without being able to demonstrate. It is also true that my use of an exercise may have departed from its originator's intent. But Jean Dasté departed from Charles Dullin, who departed from Jacques Copeau, who departed from François Delsarte, who disagreed with Jean-Gaspard Debureau, who forgot exactly what his father said, and so on through the ages. These are fluid concepts that I hope will continue to grow and metamorphose from teacher to student. As with any performing art, it's always best to learn from a real person. But it is also important to build a written legacy. There is very little documentation of people who *teach* physical comedy. I worry that the information age will somehow overlook several thousand years of master-to-student tradition. Performer-from-performer theft is important, and live opportunities have diminished of late. Vaudeville had a brief renaissance in the street theater of the sixties and seventies, but the original performers are almost gone now. The Internet doesn't lend itself well to the breeding of physical talent. Humor is far more essential to humanity's survival than the speed of our hard drives, so it seems to me that the teaching of comedy deserves some documentation.

I do believe the information age will reach a saturation point where live theater is again in great demand, providing people with human contact, inspiration, and relief from computer screens. Good comedy will be needed as long as there is something to laugh about. Hopefully this book will be of some benefit to you and to future students of the art of physical comedy. Find a way to make this work your own. Get up on your feet and try falling down. If you fail, you're halfway there. If you figure out how to react to it, you're ready to take it on the road and carry on the grand tradition of being lousy as only you know how.

···1· Preparation

To begin with, there is the space. The moment you enter a theater, a classroom, or a studio, impressions are registering consciously and subconsciously that are going to affect your work. Every action you take is affected by the constant bombardment of your senses, filtered through your intellect, emotional drives, physical needs, and memories. Is the space dark, is it airy, does it have high ceilings? How does the architecture create places of interest to you? Are you tired, hungry, lonely, alert? Are you excited by the space, are you relaxed by it, are you afraid of it? Every action you take in a workshop or a performance will be colored by these forces, until training and acts of the imagination can overcome the external and internal givens and create circumstances of your own choosing and sculpting. Space on its own is ambiguous. It is how we shape space that makes it majestic or threatening, an airy cathedral or a dingy cell. The goal in a performance is to pare away extraneous elements and use all your powers to evoke a specific image, mood, or event.

Pause. Are you holding tension anywhere as you read this? Listen. What sounds were you unaware of just now? Roll your head around. What tensions in your body were you unaware of in the last ten minutes? When was the last time you enjoyed a good, deep breath?

Actors need to be able to enter the space in a state of readiness. Their job is like a concert pianist's, whose physical, mental, and emotional awareness is finely tuned to the moment before striking the first note, whether delicate or crashing. Performers do their best work when they enter the space or an exercise in an open, alert state with a minimum of physical tension. They are ready to go in any direction. Just as the scientist in the laboratory changes one variable at a time and looks to see what the results are, the actor in an exercise must be careful not to contaminate the results by using faulty equipment. Chronic tension and personal habits can interfere with your ability as an expressive instrument to "hit all the overtones," to communicate in the richest way possible. True play comes about by actors seeing, hearing, and reacting fully to each other. The vibration of those actions must radiate out to the audience. Beginners often bring a whole repertoire of personal mannerisms, excess tension, and inarticulate phrasing to their work. At the Lecoq school in Paris, students spend months using neutral masks, biomechanics, and working with the elements to arrive at a physical, mental, and emotional state of readiness. Before you begin working, it's a good idea to spend at least a few minutes loosening up, energizing, and dropping excess tension. Warm up the body and voice so that you have an available instrument at your disposal. Even five or ten minutes of preparation will help focus your work. These are simple exercises I often return to.

Walking–Running–Pausing

Many variations of this warm-up can be found in dance and theater classes. Actively weaving through space with a large group of people quickly turns into a complex improvisation. On the simplest level, you are getting the circulation going, raising the energy level, and heightening everyone's awareness of the space, each other, and his or her impulses. Some teachers refer to this kind of walking warm-up as "milling and seething."

- Walk briskly around the room, keep your eyes on the horizon, and notice details. Leave the shoulders relaxed and the chest open, breathe easily, and keep a low center of gravity. Walk quietly. Change directions often, vary the speed of your stride, go backward or sideways, and run when possible. Work toward maximum energy with minimum effort. If in a large group, use the spaces between people and go out to the open space on the perimeter of the room. Pick up the pace. Pause suddenly and quietly without rocking forward or backward. Pause often, without letting the shoulders, neck, and lungs lock up.

VARIATIONS

- Try making eye contact or shaking hands with each person in the room as he or she passes by.

- Have everyone walk/run in geometric patterns: circles, squares, triangles, etc. Combine several patterns at the same time. Pause or change direction whenever necessary to avoid collisions. When you make eye contact passing someone, tell him or her what pattern you are walking, learn his or her pattern, and trade off.

- Call out numbers from one to seven in any order, one being the slowest and seven the fastest. Have everyone instantly shift the speed of his or her walk to the number called out. Play with contrasts.

- Call out numbers from one to six while people are walking and have everyone pause in a group of that size. Add a geometric shape to the pause, i.e. three to a circle (groups of three form a circle), or six to a square. Try to form the groups while simultaneously distributing the shapes evenly throughout the space.

- Have everyone secretly choose someone he or she is afraid of, without saying whom it is. Keep moving and stay as far away from that person as possible.

- Choose one person to focus on. Always know where he or she is as you move around the room. Add a second person, and be aware of two people at once. Add a third, then a fourth.

- Play with contact and weight exchanges, traveling around the space with a partner. Stay in physical contact the whole time. Vary the way in which you stay in contact: shoulder to shoulder, back to back, hands around shoulders, and so on. Try some lifts.

- Start in contact with one partner, travel, then break contact and trade partners with other pairs.

- Play off a partner by maintaining eye contact without ever touching. Stretch the space between you, get as far away from each other as possible, then as close together. Vary speed, height (rolling, crawling, squatting, tiptoeing), and direction while avoiding collisions with other partnerships.

• Start solo, travel, then change other people's trajectories and your own using physical contact. Jonathan Wolken of Pilobolus calls this "traffic-copping." Look for smooth ways of steering someone in a new direction that may change your own direction. Absorb someone's momentum; transform a collision into a new direction by using the back, the torso, and the hands as shock absorbers. Use pauses. Make all contact soft so that no one is jolted or tossed abruptly. Guide and be guided, so that no one is always leading or being led.

Roll Downs

Stand with your feet parallel and roll down your spine, dropping from the head first until you are hanging over at the waist, then roll back up. Do this with sound or without, with eyes open. Exhale going down, inhale coming up. Breathe into the feet as you roll up so as not to carry excess tension into the chest and shoulders. For variations, blow through the lips on a descending scale while rolling down, inhale, and blow through on an ascending scale on the way back up. Another variation is to roll up with an undulation. Hang over at the waist. Begin the roll up on an inhale by bending the legs and pushing the knees forward, then ripple up through the hips, chest, and head. Keep your heels on the floor, distributing your weight evenly on the whole foot during the entire ripple. Once you are standing, bend over at the waist with a flat back, bringing your arms forward on an exhale until you are hanging over and ready for the next ripple up.

Moving on a Breath

Walk on an exhale. With your eyes on the horizon, stand still while inhaling, turn the head in a new direction. As you begin to exhale, start traveling on your breath in the direction you are facing. Stop as soon as you run out of air. Inhale, turn your head in a new direction, and repeat the cycle. Let the quality of your breathing be reflected in the quality of your traveling movement. Vary the dynamics: Try slow exhales, puffs, and long exhales, matched with jumps, runs, and slow walks. Add sound on the exhale while traveling.

Spatial Awareness

Define your awareness of space with your arms, and see how it affects you. Put both arms straight out and parallel in front of you. Travel as if this were all you could see, with a very tight, narrow focus. Move around the room, lower the arms, and maintain that narrow focus. Try a different sense of space. Hold your arms wide open on a high diagonal, as if blessing the sky. Travel around the room without looking down. Lower the arms and maintain that focus. How does it affect you? Do diagonal-down, vertical, horizontal-wide, etc. It will be clear even from doing this exercise as a warm-up how much character is a result of your sense of space—some of these positions will feel happy, others businesslike.

Center of Gravity

Explore centers of gravity. Stand parallel and lean forward slightly so that all your weight is in front of you. Keep your weight to the front and walk, sit, stand, do every action you can think of while *always* maintaining that center of gravity. Then shift your weight behind you and do the same pattern of actions with your new center of gravity. Finally, try all of the above actions with your weight perfectly centered. Make a mental note of where you habitually tend to carry your weight. Note the emotional and psychological states various centers of gravity tend to provoke, for example, weight forward: anxious and busy; weight backward: tired, lazy, resistant, etc. Work over time toward being centered, relaxed, and ready to move in any direction without carrying chronic imbalances into every exercise.

Low Center Grounding

I call these "Ha's." Do a little jog around the room. Every seven or eight steps, jump and land quietly in a low wide second, planting both feet firmly on the ground. As you land, open the arms wide, focus in that direction, and say "Ha" on an exhale. Vary the direction of your focus and the width of your arms. Alternate extending the arms on horizontal, vertical, and diagonal planes. Practice keeping the shoulders down while reaching. Alternate between doing Ha's to people and places close to you, and Ha's to the far side of the room. Vary the length and attack of the sound, from extended to staccato. Combine the Ha's with the walking–running–pausing pedestrian warm-ups. Remember to land quietly with a minimum of tension. Land with feet flat on the floor, use a low center of gravity that stops all momentum with no wobbling. Collect your energy and radiate strength from the ground through the legs, up the torso, and out through the arms and eyes into space. I find this particularly useful for warming up cast members before a performance.

Leg Articulators

Do little knee exchanges, loosening up the joints (as if pedaling a bicycle) by raising the heels while keeping your toes on the ground. Keep the head level. Do it with feet parallel, then repeat with feet turned out. Stay in the turned out position and go into a small run, picking up the feet and lifting the knees high while still keeping the head level. Do a sequence of triplets, stepping left–right–left, and pause with your knee in the air. Hold it for a beat to mark the end of that movement, then do another triplet so that you mark the end of the phrase with your other knee in the air. This not only gets you warmed up, it adds definition to your movements.

Sharpening the Senses

Sight

Notice the room. Travel around the room, making note of how long you focus on something and how often you shift your focus. Try looking at things from a new perspective by tilting your head and looking down the length of the wall or lying on the floor and looking at the ceiling. Extend the amount of time you focus on one point, travel to it, and pick a new point. Try a stream of consciousness monologue while continuing to explore visually, giving voice to the impulses stirred up. Make eye contact with someone and never break it, traveling toward and away from him or her in constant response to the other person's actions.

Sound

Hear the sounds in the room, outside the room, and the sounds you make. Play with impulses based on noises farthest from you and closest to you. Use your voice—explore your personal palette of sounds, without dialogue. Play with moving while making sounds. Get a partner; have your partner close his or her eyes. Make a little identifiable noise that you repeat like a beacon. Move away from your partner and see if he or she can follow with eyes closed (no physical contact). Lead your partner around the room by having him or her follow your sound. If other pairs are playing, move away from your partners and see if they can find you by listening for your sound amid everyone else's.

Smell

Smell your clothes, each other, the environment. Describe imagined smells out loud that have a visceral impact on you and each other. Have everyone close his or her eyes. Think of evocative smells, call them out one at a time, and have everyone do a short movement phrase in reaction to the smell. What parts of your body respond to different smells? Pace the calling out to give players time to absorb each smell. Use pleasant images as well as unpleasant ones. Let different people call out smells so that no one person dominates the suggestions.

Taste

Successful actors are people who have a love for the "taste" of language. They know how to relish each word, to chew each sound, and to spit out an insult. Choose a word you like; repeat it over and over, embellishing and embodying the full flavor of each syllable. Put a movement phrase on each sound. Pick a new word. State out loud things you enjoy or dislike tasting. Take turns around the room, with everyone doing a quick movement response to each image mentioned. Try improvising the description of a fabulous meal, from beginning to end. Have a conversation with a partner about the most luscious thing you could eat right now. Embellish each other's images and use as much vocal and physical coloring as possible.

TOUCH

Contact all of the different surfaces in the space: walls, windows, floors, pipes, each other—anything that doesn't hurt. Use different parts of the body to make contact. I had a mountain-climbing friend who believed you couldn't really experience the summit of a climb without rolling in the dirt at the top. Bring someone to a surface that feels interesting. Go feel what others found interesting. Improvise different ways of making contact with someone. Go from familiar points of contact to less familiar. Tapping the shoulders, hugging, or walking hand in hand are familiar. Try standing sideways hip to hip or hugging a partner's calf. Play with different degrees of density, weight, and time. Travel impulsively with someone while staying in touch; join other pairs or individuals, trading off on different points of contact. Explore impulses, but keep it safe: Don't hurt anyone! Remember, it's just a warm-up. Get a partner, stand behind him or her and gently push through different parts of his or her body. Partners should move like a blade of grass that bends in the breeze and returns to standing. Try pushing through your partner's head, shoulders, hips, and arms with no predictable pattern. Be careful not to jolt your partner; make soft points of contact.

···2·Solos

This chapter covers exercises that can be done by one person: classic bits, physical reactions, impersonations, improvisations, and studies with objects and obstacles. There are many ways of doing them with other people, but the basic structures do not require any assistance. You can do them in large groups or one at a time, but do use an audience as often as possible while doing the exercises. The more opportunities actors have to feel the pulse of working in public, the better.

The first few actions are classic gags that have been around forever: trips, kicks, and falls. They make a succinct starting point for entering the world of physical comedy because they are simple to see and hard to do well. Approach, execution, and follow-through are all there in a nutshell. Telegraphing, tension, missed footing, and other problems that beginners often have are easy to see. Learning a well-executed trip teaches basic principles that serve one well when developing more complex patterns.

Another set of principles worth being aware of are Newton's laws of motion. Whether audiences know it or not, the laws guide their expectations of any action. Here they are:

1. **A body at rest tends to stay at rest or a body in motion tends to stay in motion in a straight line and at a constant speed, unless acted upon by an outside force.** Warner Brothers cartoons frequently play with expectations based on this principle, as in delaying a fall when Daffy Duck runs off a cliff.

2. **The acceleration of a mass by a force is directly proportional to the force and inversely proportional to the mass.** If a big lug gets hit on the head with a frying pan and doesn't flinch, then the audience can't avoid feeling that the pan-wielder is about to get crushed by the lug.

3. **For every action there is an equal and opposite reaction.** This is the most important law in theater to be aware of. Break this, or the law of gravity, and audiences go nuts.

The Trip

ACTION

You walk across the room at a healthy clip. Without changing your stride in any detectable way or planning when it will happen, you surprise yourself by tripping. You react and recover your stride.

TECHNIQUE

In real life, you trip most often by not paying attention to where you are walking. You stub your foot on an uneven surface like a rock, a crack, a hole, a root, or a curb. On stage, the best way to simulate a trip is to stumble over your own feet. While walking, rotate the ankle of the back leg as it comes off the floor so that your toes and the top part of your foot just catch the back heel of your forward foot. This will jolt you out of the rhythm of your walk and produce a trip. Take care not to put added force into the back foot when hitting your heel—it hurts. Try to just catch the top side of your toes as your foot passes by in its stride. Be careful not to stub your toes against your heel. Twist your foot so that your toe joints line up with your other foot's Achilles' tendon. Wear sneakers that protect your feet while you are learning this little move. Catch your weight with one stride as you fall forward, landing on the same leg that caught against the heel. In extreme cases, the situation might call for you to take the fall all the way to the floor (see the sections on falls later in this chapter). I've also seen people with new sneakers able to catch the fresh rubber on the floor and produce a real trip, which you may want to try if the ankle-hook method doesn't work for you.

PITFALLS

It's trickier than it sounds. The automatic safety reflexes of the body will want to engage, usually by slowing your rear leg down as it brushes by the heel the moment just before you trip yourself. To an audience, this gives the move away and robs it of its spontaneity, a mistake that is oftentimes called telegraphing. Until you have made the move second nature through practice, the eyes also have a nasty way of letting the audience know you are thinking about tripping, rather than focusing on a task at hand that a trip interrupts. I call it the "learner's glaze."

Ideally, a physical ripple passes through the body equivalent to the force of the trip. Beginners often overreact to the amount of force in the follow-through or become rigid. This is a good example of needing Newton's third law: For every action there is an equal and opposite reaction. Stay relaxed. Don't let your enthusiasm carry you into a run that smashes into the opposite wall, unless you've carefully practiced the collision. Your arms, torso, and head should swing easily in direct proportion to the amount of shock caused by the trip. If it's just a little trip, your body should respond gently; more force, more response. You need to let your body really go a little off balance for your reactions to be believable, but there is no need to hurt yourself by going too far. Be consistent with the rhythm of your walk on the approach.

Once you master the basic technique and can do it out of a brisk walk, perfect the psychological moment of catching yourself by surprise. Put your focus on some other time, place, or person during the approach so that you trip yourself without revealing the moment the imbalance will occur. If you feel the moment start to telegraph, don't do it then. Keep walking until you can surprise yourself. Give your foot an independent brain, the same way you scratch yourself unconsciously while thinking about something else. You almost have to induce a state of dual personality, where you are both consciously a magician taking the audience's focus elsewhere and unconsciously the person who's being fooled. There was a great episode on the Dick Van Dyke show where Rob did a demonstration for little Richie's school on what makes comedy work. It's a masterful demonstration of misdirection and how to surprise people by consciously setting them up to expect something and then invisibly doing the unexpected.

VARIATIONS

The simple action of tripping says many different things, depending on your timing, energy level, pauses, use of space, and emotional and psychological choices. Change the tempo of the walk. Vary the moment when the trip occurs: early on, midstride, or just before getting to your destination. You may feel no different as a person manipulating one of these elements, but to an audience watching you, it becomes clear how much character *is* action. After mastering the technique of tripping, play with the most important variable: the reaction. As Bill Irwin says, "It really isn't the trip itself that's funny. It's the gestures and motions afterwards, the looking back at the spot, the trying to make an excuse for having tripped." Play with a variety of reactions. This process of trying out possibilities broadens your range and helps you refine your own comic persona. Character is revealed by the way in which people deal with the loss of dignity caused by a trip. Try each of the following reactions and see which ones you identify with most. Invent your own. The trip is the action; what you do with it is the reaction. If you don't execute an *honest* trip, you will have a *false* reaction. Make sure you don't react before you act, the old walk into a room and pick up the phone before it rings action because that was your cue. Stay in the present, and don't wait for the phone to ring.

Here are some common scenarios. They all illustrate some human trait you might recognize. Keep your facial expressions simple, and don't overdo selling your choice. In all this work, avoid excess "mugging" (making faces to attract attention). Trust that your body language and internal psychological state will reveal all.

The action is described first, the train of thought is in parenthesis.

- Walk briskly, trip, pause without looking back, and continue brisk walk. (What just happened?)
- Look around to see if anyone saw you. (Was anyone looking?)
- Admit you're clumsy, turn, and bow for everyone to see. (You got me. I'm such a klutz!)
- Trip, turn around, point, and blame the spot on the ground you tripped on. (It wasn't my fault!)

- Trip, pause, and enjoy it. Go back and trip again at the same spot. Repeat and accelerate. (That was fun!)
- Incorporate the trip into the rhythm of your walk as if you meant to do that. (I was just dancing, la di da.)
- Deny the truth. Use your whole body to deny the fact as soon as you trip. Regain your composure and regular rhythm immediately. (I didn't trip.)
- Once people have seen you trip at a certain spot, appear to be very clever by jumping over the spot, then trip immediately afterwards. (I outsmarted you—ooops!)

The Flying Hat

ACTION

You take a fedora, derby, or other hat, and start to place it on your head. Just as you pull it down, it flies off your head by some magical force.

TECHNIQUE

Put your middle finger on your thumb and flick it sharply as if you were shooting a marble. This is what launches the hat. Place your fingers on each side of the rim of the hat, slipping your middle fingers under the rim. Raise the hat high above your head so that the direction of the hat going on your head is straight down. Just at the moment it would land snugly, flick your fingers so that the hat flies up.

PITFALLS

This action works best as one smooth sequence, so that the force of the hat going down appears to be the cause of the hat flying up. If you take the tiniest of beats to rearrange your fingers for the flick while putting the hat on, you destroy the effect. Some hats work better than others. It needs to be light enough to get some altitude off the little flick and stiff enough to respond. Practice picking it up so that the fingers are perfectly positioned each time. Like the trip, stay in the present. Go into the action knowing the hat is on your head until the moment of discovery occurs. W. C. Fields was a master at this, as was Chaplin.

VARIATIONS

The moment of the flying hat is more in the supernatural realm than the human foible category. When done right, it looks like the hat is misbehaving. This can lead into a whole cascade of hat manipulations. If hats interest you, know that some people have made whole careers out of virtuoso hat moves. In juggling literature, you can find extensive descriptions of hat spins, rolls, catches, and tosses. Some people do these variations as if they were very clumsy. Others choreograph routines as graceful as Fred Astaire dancing with a broom. For our purposes, try this one simple action, then explore reactions by going back through the same variables used in trips: space, tempo, energy levels, and emotional and psychological foibles. In this case, character is revealed by how you deal with the unknown.

- An easy variation to play with once you have mastered the technique is to not notice the hat is missing. Carry on a bit until you feel its absence or see it lying on the ground. Jacques Lecoq believes that "the comic effect occurs when one follows through to the succeeding actions before realizing that an error has been made. The longer it takes to realize the error, the denser the character is."

The Hat Kick

ACTION

You see a hat on the ground, walk over to pick it up, and just as you get there it flies away. When it stops moving, you go over to pick it up, and again it flies away.

TECHNIQUE

This is related to the action of the flying hat, both in execution and in its supernatural appearance. You propel the hat with your toe just as your hands reach for it, giving the illusion that the reach is causing the hat's flight. To hide the fact that you are actually kicking it, your downstage foot steps in front of the hat as you walk over to it, blocking the audience's view for a second. Your other foot snaps in place right next to the downstage foot, kicking the hat.

PITFALLS

The foot that kicks the hat shouldn't go beyond the foot that is planted downstage. Practice the move without a hat, just taking a few steps and then stopping, scuffing the other foot into place on the floor next to the planted foot. Your momentum on the walk needs to stop clearly as you reach for the hat and kick it at the same time. Otherwise, it will look as if you are chasing and kicking the hat yourself. Often while learning this move, you may accidentally step on the rim and trap the hat, instead of sending it flying. When this happens, the game is over; pick up the hat and put it on, rather than pretend it can still be kicked. The moment has passed. Start over. Keep the toe of the kicking foot low to the ground, almost sliding it on the floor, so that the hat rim can't get between your toe and the floor.

VARIATIONS

Play with pauses. Remember that it is your reaction to the hat flying away that makes the move interesting. Do the flying hat and follow it with the hat kick.

- Try pausing when you're standing over the hat before you reach for it and bring the other leg in.
- Pause while the hat is traveling, look at it till it stops, and formulate your next approach.
- Sneak up and dive on the hat to stop it. Bill Irwin does a diving forward handspring into the hat, coming up with it on his head. He's also a good enough performer to put such a big move in context. Fabulous moves done just to show off quickly turn into boring demonstrations of technique.

The Pie in the Face

It never was funny in the first place. Gags like these give comedy a bad name. Maybe you'll be the one to find a way to make it work.

Pratfalls

Buster Keaton is the master of pratfalls. The total abandon with which he throws himself into a wall, the floor, and midair is a priceless work of art. He was also raised since childhood to do pratfalls and still managed to fracture his neck, so don't try those moves at home. They hurt. Don't let anyone tell you otherwise: Those old-timers took some very hard knocks. If you have access to gym mats, combat padding, and a foam landing pit, you might try some of the more complex moves seen in silent movies. I am only going to cover a few of the less spectacular falls that are useful as a follow-through to when you trip, slip, or are off balance. Most actors perform on hard, wooden floors, not sand or other more yielding surfaces, so be careful. It's not worth injuring yourself for the sake of a little extra believability.

The Scissors Kick Fall

ACTION

You are kicked in the butt or tripped, slip on a banana peel, or hear a loud noise. Your legs fly up in the air, and you land on the floor in a sitting position.

TECHNIQUE

You can do this fall from a standing position or a calm walk. It requires no momentum, as the direction of the fall is up before you go down. The action of the legs and arms communicates the magnitude of the fall. Start the fall by splaying your arms out as if opening a set of curtains. Kick your right leg straight up and hop off the floor with your left leg, so that it looks as if the right leg carried your body up. If you're left-handed, you may want to start with the other leg instead. As you are going up in the air, quickly bring your left leg up so that for one brief moment both your legs are in the air in front of you. Instead of letting gravity do its job and landing on your butt, break your fall with your right leg and lower your weight down to the floor. Lean slightly onto your left buttock as you land on the floor so that you don't injure your spine. Slap the floor with your hands when you land to increase the sound of the impact. Do this slowly at first, gradually increasing the pace to create a more believable fall. The trick is in practicing until you perfect the ability to distribute your weight very quickly.

PITFALLS

It's hard to practice this fall without getting a sore leg. You are actually putting your right foot on the floor and lowering your weight quickly instead of falling, so your leg is bound to get tired. Never lose control of your weight. The illusion is to lower yourself almost as fast as an actual fall. Make sure you roll out onto your left buttock to disperse the weight, rather than just thudding. You may be able to go straight down and get more of a thud effect if you use your hands to break the fall. Whether you are kicked, surprised, or slip, remember to amplify the fall with the arms and legs—it pulls the audience's eye away from the leg that briefly supports you. Be careful with slipping not to actually slip. Unlike the trip, where you really do want to go off balance, the scissors kick requires you have control over your weight when you jump up. An actual slip will throw off your ability to jump up and highly increase the chance that you will crash onto your spine or your head and cause serious injury.

VARIATIONS

Landing on your butt is good for certain reactions. You can also roll out onto your back and end up with your feet in the air for a different effect. It all depends on the action that precedes the fall. Try reacting to a loud noise or slipping on something on the floor, and see which end position feels right. Because this is such a large, final move, it does tend to be the end of a phrase rather than the beginning of a sequence.

The Backward Fall

ACTION

You take a step backward and fall to the ground.

TECHNIQUE

Like the scissors kick fall, again you control your own weight all the way to the floor; gravity should never add to the momentum. As you step back with your right leg (again, you may reverse this by starting on the left), lean forward at the waist and lower yourself until the left buttock touches the floor. Continue distributing the fall along the floor by rolling out along your left side, keeping your head and neck up so as not to injure them. Add to the sound of the impact by slapping the floor as you roll out. You can use the leg to add to the counterbalancing effect of your descent by rotating onto the outside of your left heel as you step back with your right foot. As you lower your weight, the side of your left leg stays in contact with the floor and can begin the weight transfer, which then rolls through the butt and out onto your left side.

PITFALLS

Make sure you bend forward as you step backward. This distributes your weight over your right foot and lowers your center of gravity safely to the floor. Be careful not to twist your right ankle or land on it on your way down.

VARIATIONS

- Again, the variations are in the preceding action. This move works well from being shoved, hitting a wall or pillar and stumbling backward, being drunk, etc. This fall can have a softer landing than the scissors kick, so some actions may call for you to get up and go back into the fray, only to fall again. You can make it a more final move by adding to the illusion of pain or passing flat out on the floor.
- Try falling over the shoulder. You can continue the momentum of any backward fall into a backward shoulder roll. Continue

contracting as you sit out on the fall, place your left arm out to the side for balance, and do a left-side shoulder roll, ending up laying out with your face down.

- Buster Keaton does a fabulous head-spin variation. After falling backward, he rolls up into a headstand and, while balancing on his head, spins himself around and flops straight over. Good luck, and *ouch*.

Forward Fall

ACTION

You walk into a room, trip, and fall flat on your face.

TECHNIQUE

This is harder than falling backward. You are creating the illusion of landing on your face without really doing so. The same principle of controlling your own descent by counterbalancing and taking the weight through your thigh to the floor applies, but there are more ways to get injured falling forward. Do this slowly at first, and never let your enthusiasm exceed your control. Take a big step forward with your right leg and lower your weight toward the floor. Counterbalance the descent by extending your left leg backward, turning in on the instep and starting the weight transfer into the floor. Keep your right leg opened out to the side so that you aren't coming down on your kneecap. If you push your stomach out and curve your body like a banana so that the force of the fall turns into a rocking-chair action, nothing will get bruised. Hold your head up, away from hitting the floor, and use your forearms and hands to cushion your landing.

PITFALLS

Most people injure themselves by banging a knee or elbow on their fall. Keep the angle of the weight transfer running through the "meaty" side of your muscle groups, not your bones. Use the calves, thighs, abdomen, and forearms. Another common injury is floor burn. Even if you distribute the fall properly to the floor, excess momentum can cause you to keep sliding once you are down. I've seen people scrape their hands, feet, and forearms because they didn't check their speed going into the fall. If you want to slide, make sure you have checked the surface and are wearing protective clothing. Failure to hold the head safely through the move can result in a banged chin or a bit tongue.

VARIATIONS

- Like the backward fall, a forward fall can be converted into a shoulder roll. You can also turn a front fall into a side fall, distributing the impact along either side of the body. Instead of sprawling to the front with the knee out to the side like a bent swastika, a side fall leaves you lying on the floor like a log. Modern dancers use this move all the time to go to the floor. It starts with the left arm swinging across the body and out along the floor. Place the instep of your left foot behind the right foot, and begin transferring weight to the floor. Lean over to the right to counterbalance as you descend, and slide your weight along the floor on the palm of your left hand. Lower yourself with your right leg and use your right hand in front of you for support. The side fall, done without the arm swinging, is very effective for fainting.

- Try a dead fall to the front. With a little practice, you can pike slightly and break your fall with your hands as you go straight over. I've also seen a few experts go up on their toes and arc their whole body like a crescent moon, absorbing the impact like a rocking chair. This is very difficult!

Corkscrews

ACTION

You hop on your left leg while your right leg spins in a circle, then hop onto the right leg while your left leg spins in a circle.

TECHNIQUE

This is an old vaudeville move that you often see Groucho Marx or Buster Keaton do; it was probably handed down from English pantomimes and earlier comics. Try to see it on film, video, or in person before learning it. Groucho does it in *Animal Crackers* while singing "Hooray for Captain Spaulding," Buster does it in *The Playhouse*. Most people feel quite klutzy doing it until they can speed the action up and blur the legs into an illusion of circular motion. The higher you raise the circling leg, the better. Baggy pants help the look of it.

Hop twice on each foot. On the first hop, extend your free leg out to the side with your toes angled down. On the second hop you do the corkscrew *while* changing direction to set up the next arabesque. It's easier to learn if you start in the middle of the move. Stand on your turned-out right leg, knee slightly bent and over your toes, body facing to the right and upright. Lift the left leg straight out to the side as high as you can, toes pointing down and heel up. Don't twist your standing leg knee joint. Keeping your thigh up, draw a circle with your heel, rotating at the knee joint. Go in first to your butt with your heel, then rotate your knee up to the sky so that the heel can continue its action around and out, leaving your leg in a kick-to-the-side position. You are now facing left. All this happens quickly on one hop, so that when your heel comes around into the kick, your balance leg can rotate from turned out to turned in, and no strain is put on the supporting knee. Your body will want to turn from facing right to facing left as your leg circles. Now hop onto your left foot (the kicking foot), facing left, while your right leg extended out in an arabesque with heel up. Begin the next corkscrew *and* hop on your left leg for the second time, changing direction once again with your leg and body. Hop back onto the right leg, and you are at the end of one full phrase.

PITFALLS

There is a definite rhythm to this move that creates the illusion of legs spinning in a circle. To get the most circular motion, you need to cheat to the side with your hips while keeping your head, neck, and chest facing front; you need to use your gluteal muscles to lift the leg high. You must be careful not to twist the knee of your supporting leg. The hop is partly to give a rhythm to the leg circle, but also to shift directions so that the knee joint doesn't twist when you change sides. If you keep your supporting knee over the ball of your foot and don't hop, you can feel the right place to change direction. The circling heel starts towards the butt before you hop/change direction. When it can go no further, the whole leg has to rotate, which changes the angle of inclination of the aerial leg and forces the supporting leg to rotate at the same time. Do it standing still, then practice doing it on a hop.

VARIATIONS

This move can be used to change directions while crossing the stage or to put a flourish on the end of a kicking action. If you make an exit and leave a leg up behind you in arabesque, you can do one corkscrew to bring the body around and walk in the opposite direction.

- Corkscrews can also be done in a more parallel position, with less changing of direction from side to side. You can make the leg doing the corkscrew end up in front, and appear to kick the standing leg into the air behind you, which launches the next corkscrew. It's as if the falling leg kicks the next leg into action, with the illusion that you will fall over if the legs don't keep spinning.

Head Slams

ACTION

You go to leave a room, open a door, and slam your head on the door as you open it.

TECHNIQUE

Choose your door wisely. Some work well, others have no effect. All you have to do is face the door and place your foot closer to the door than your head. Hit your foot instead of your head when you swing the door open. Wear shoes! Bend your toes up, if possible, so that the door is hitting the ball of your foot. Snap your head back when the door hits your foot, cover your forehead with your hands, and mime extreme pain. The hand that isn't on the doorknob can also make contact with the door at the same time as the foot, to add to the sound of the collision while protecting the head at the same time. Hide the illusion by using the foot and hand most upstage to the audience.

PITFALLS

Some doors just don't work. They have to be light enough to swing quickly so that the door hits your foot with a sharp smack and sturdy enough to withstand the shock without hurting your foot or breaking the door. Avoid the temptation to kick at the door—the audience will see it. Focus should stay on the upper half of your body. Practice by placing your foot a few inches away from the door in its closed position, making sure your body is safely behind the stopping point set up by your foot. You don't have to open the door very far for it to be effective, you just have to do it quickly in one, clean snap. If the door is too heavy you'll hurt your toes and miss out on the nice whacking sound.

VARIATIONS

- Instead of taking the door to you, you can also take yourself to the door or a wall or pillar. Use a door or a wall that is hollow enough to have some resonance, and slap it with the palm of your hand. Solid concrete is too dense; plywood or drywall works well, just don't overdo the slap. Use the upstage hand to slap the wall for the sound of the impact, preferably down by your side where it is less noticeable. Walk straight into the wall or door, snapping your head back as you slap it for the sound of impact. Keep your head back six to eight inches from the real point of impact, puffing your chest out a little to absorb the impact should you miscalculate. Again use the upstage hand. Once you are adept at simultaneously timing the head snap, the sound from the slap, and stopping your momentum from the walk, build up to doing it from a run.
- You can run backward and turn around at the right moment, giving the illusion of not seeing the door coming. A really devastating collision would end with a slow slide down to the floor, the proverbial birdies-circling-the-head knockout.

The Take

Comedy is in the pauses. Pausing is not always a natural rhythm, but it is a technique that can be learned. Pausing allows the performer to build a train of thought and gives the audience time to see what that train of thought is. It also keeps the performer open to the environment and allows a true reaction to build. It allows the audience entrance into the actor's psychology. The director George Abbott defined comedy as the derailing of a train of thought. Abbott says the moment of derailing should always be marked by a pause, no matter how slight. If you were to slam your thumb with a hammer in real life, you would cry and rush to get medical treatment. If you were to mime that action on stage for comic effect, you could pause the moment after you hit it (take 1), tilt your head up to the audience to think (take 2), then move forward into any sequence of actions that play off that first moment of impact. Eventually the pain might show up through a scream, through your legs, or any other channel from minuscule to enormous. The length of the pause, and how the actor reacts, is what begins to differentiate one performer from another.

One of the biggest dangers with people working in comedy is the belief that they have to make their reactions funny. It is equivalent to believing that you need to sound Shakespearean to act Shakespeare. This is simply naive. It's not a question of scale or style. Some moments may require huge facial/physical reactions because it is absolutely the only way to make the moment believable. Other times, subtlety is the best answer. I try to get students to play with the whole spectrum. Take something to the extreme, then take it to the minimal. The difference between psychological acting and working in a comic universe is that in comedy, the psychological life of the character must somehow manifest itself physically, even in stillness. This is true in most forms of acting, but in physical comedy the use of time, space, and energy can go far beyond the conventional limits of realistic choices. Isolate different parts of the body, and react only with the hands, only with the feet, or only with the torso. Play with pauses longer than you would in real life. Go much closer or further away from a point of impact. Use a totally unexpected level of energy to respond to a moment of surprise. Often laughter is a cathartic reaction by audiences to the incongruity of the comic's actions. Knowing how a "normal" person would react, the comic creates unique pressures by reacting in unexpected ways that can only be relieved by laughter. It's a case of taking advantage of our assumptions of how the universe works. Even when these imbalances are created, I believe they still obey internal laws of motion and harmony when they succeed, but that's a topic for another book.

The Five Dollar Bill

ACTION

You preset a five dollar bill on the stage. You make an entrance, walk past it, and react.

TECHNIQUE

This action is open to many variations. Make a choice beforehand and explore one variable at a time. Try starting with the head, and work your way down. First choose a specific walk. Go across the stage, pass the five dollar bill, and pause. React with the head. This could be as small as just thinking you saw something, changing your mind, and continuing without looking back, to doing a huge double take with the head and going back to the bill and stealing it. Repeat this cross several times, initiating reactions with only the hands, only the feet, and so on. Vary the length of the pauses. Vary the tempo of the walk on your entrance. Play with huge reactions and stone-faced reactions. Play with everything from walking way beyond the bill to noticing it before you walk past it. Walk by and pick it up in one continuous cross. Then try combining these elements.

PITFALLS

This is a diagnostic exercise, designed to give people an appreciation for all the variables they have at their fingertips. It also gives reactions greater physical life and clarity. Try everything you can think of. This is a good exercise to do in front of an audience. It gives you feedback on what choices work. One problem with learning more about your comic persona is that you are quite often the last to know what really works best. If you have a habit of mugging or not using enough physical energy, your most natural choices may feel right to you but may, in fact, be blocking your comic development.

- Once you have played with separate reactions using the legs, torso, hands, and head, make up combinations. Decide ahead of time on an order: legs–torso–head or hands–legs–hands. The five dollar bill exercise is also a metaphor for any moment of discovery; it could just as easily be a reaction to another person, something horrible, or something frightening. Play with putting different objects on stage. Put the actor in the wings and have someone else preset the stage without the actor seeing, so you can be sure of an honest reaction. Use something mysterious, like a box or bag, which may contain something else inside it. Ultimately, the audience itself can become the object the actor is reacting to. Stay honest, be patient, and let the actions and reactions between performer and audience resonate. See the exercises under Difficulty with Objects.

- Two people can do this at the same time, playing a complex game of Ping-Pong (see Chapter 3) while trying to resolve what happens to the bill.

Impersonating the Masters

During the Renaissance, when painting students apprenticed with a master, they learned how to paint by imitating the master's brush strokes, sometimes spending years copying the same subject over and over. This is also very useful in the field of physical comedy. It was how all the great comics learned. Stan Laurel and Charlie Chaplin apprenticed with the same troupe: the Karno Company from England. Fortunately for us, some of their examples survive on film and video. Spend an afternoon copying a Groucho song and dance or Chaplin's elegant counterpoint strut, and present a classic routine with a partner or by yourself to the class. Like students of painting, this will help you to get a feel for the form and technique of physical comedy. The Marx Brothers started out by soaking up influences from their neighborhood, their relatives, and other performers. Like them, imitation can provide you with the tools needed to build your own persona.

ACTION

You learn a classic silent bit from a comic master, note for note. You practice the actor's body language, tempo, expressions, and way of thinking. If he or she speaks, you copy the dialogue exactly. You bring your research back to class and trade off demonstrating for each other the routines you've studied.

TECHNIQUE

Study routines on video in slow motion and learn them exactly. Read biographies and other source material for an understanding of how the comic worked. Most importantly, you need to intuit the inner life of your master; what drives him or her, how does he or she perceive the world? Without this inner understanding of the actor's point of view, your efforts to impersonate will be hollow and lack commitment. The more diverse the masters a student imitates, the more the student will expand his or her own physical vocabulary. Choose masters out loud in class before researching them, so that no two students study the same source material. Cross-gender casting works just fine; women should feel free to impersonate men, and men women. Useful people to cover are Chaplin, Keaton, Langdon, Lloyd, Curly, the Marx Brothers, Bert Lahr, Tati, Max Linder, Abbott and Costello, Laurel and Hardy, Jackie Gleason, Sid Ceasar, Peter Sellers, Art Carney, John Cleese, Steve Martin, Mae West, Fannie Brice, Imogene Coca, Lily Tomlin, Tracy Ullman, Lucille Ball, and Mary Tyler Moore.

PITFALLS

Sometimes people pick routines that aren't very physical. Avoid pure standup routines. Find enough film/video footage to make the study worthwhile. I've seen some pretty lame presentations with low commitment levels because there wasn't enough interest in the subject chosen. In contrast, I've seen some remarkable presentations by students who were obsessed, coming in fully costumed and rehearsed to the point where they *were* the person they were imitating. That usually has the effect of shaming the rest of the class into wanting another week to polish up their presentations. The spirit of Harpo or Lucy can live again through the work of an insightful student.

Choose at your own peril that whole genre of performer I call the child-adult. Nothing against them personally, but imitating the contortions and tension levels found in children-adults can give beginners some bad habits. Performers often found in child-adult terrain are Jerry Lewis, Pee Wee Herman, Mr. Bean, Tommy Smothers, Erkel, Chris Farley, Ed Grimley, Gilda Radner, or any comedian who uses a childlike persona. Do them sparingly; they often don't breathe while they work. Find balance by also imitating someone who breathes more.

VARIATIONS

Play follow the leader. Teach everyone in class your master's rhythms, what his or her point of view is, and his or her relationship to the environment. One at a time, reveal to everyone what shifts you had to make to embody your master and have classmates mirror you. Teach everyone part of the routine, the signature actions and thoughts, then move on. I usually only do four to five masters a day; it takes some time to learn each one and some of them are exhausting!

This exercise demonstrates how much energy the physical comedian needs to illustrate a particular train of thought: When Curly of the Three Stooges sees something on the ground, he will step over it, hop backward, hit his head, wave his arm, and stick his neck out three times. Stan Laurel works with a different rhythm—a gentle, continuous cascade of actions. Harpo is chaos in its most divine state. These many viewpoints are all inherently comic. Imitating masters is a way of nudging your own intuitive reactions into fuller physical expression.

Solo Improvisations

These improvisations are a little different from traditional who, what, where, and when exercises. There are many fine books that cover that ground in depth. These exercises focus instead on finding physical life. In some cases, the improvising is done off stage, edited, and then presented to the group. Other times, you are playing moment to moment in front of the audience. Some of these improvisations turn into full-fledged performance pieces, others are just developmental. Improvisation is a good tool for learning moment-to-moment honesty because everything really *is* happening for the first time. Reactions are true. The tricky part is transferring that sense of truth to a script or scenario with the same timing and spontaneity. In a choreographed exercise, such as succeed–succeed–fail, you use improvisation to *find* the moves that you then present to class. The timing within the set choreography is still open to improvisation, but technically, there is no writing on the spot.

In spontaneous exercises, like harangues or moments of glory, you do improvise live in front of the class to better understand the actor-audience relationship and to develop what you have to say on stage. This can be fascinating, but these improvisations are not finished performances, as in *Second City* or *Whose Line Is It Anyway*. They are for actor training, not audience edification. The main reason audiences never see these kinds of improvisation is simple: They don't have enough patience. Actors have a tremendous fear of inadequacy, of boring the audience, of not being good enough, so the act of improvisation is often colored by a performance style in which fast-thinking, cliché-ridden situations are played for easy laughs. This work requires a patient, sober audience interested in process. Fellow students usually work best.

Training improvisations take time. Most audiences aren't interested in sitting in a theater and riding out the boring parts to get to the good stuff. Be patient; you will see some remarkable things. You may even market these ideas, or use them in a show, but for now don't worry about entertainment value. Allow an improvisation to begin quietly, give it time for nothing much to happen. Rich theatrical territory will open up. The senses become finely tuned, and there is an alertness and quickening of the actor's reflexes. Impulses become totally focused on the pursuit of a theme. There is a feeling of absolute abandon and complete control, as the improvisation develops effortlessly through the actor's impeccable technique. Time stops; the audience is absorbed in something unique and ephemeral happening at exactly the moment it should. At least, that's the goal!

Harangues

The most basic thing a performer can do is enter the space and do nothing. It is the equivalent of the sentence "I am." All things begin from that point. A harangue is a structure for experimenting with simple beginnings, exploring impulses one at a time. According to the dictionary, a harangue is a loud address to a multitude of people. At the Celebration Barn Theater, it was the name of an exercise developed by Tony Montanaro. After spending several summers doing them, I can think of no better name, even though these harangues often involve no dialogue.

Actors explore time, memory, sound, mood, movement, and space. You harangue the audience, yourself, and the world, in a moment-to-moment quest for truth. It is an improv that gets at the heart of what you want to say on stage. It's not always pleasant, interesting, or entertaining. It is not geared specifically toward comedy. A harangue is a tool for working on timing, exploring interests, getting more physically expressive, and connecting to the audience. It is almost the exact opposite of Jacques Lecoq's carefully structured exercises, and more along the lines of the jump in the pool and learn how to swim philosophy. I find exposure to both schools helpful. Entrances and exits become important. Starting points are important. Like the first line of a novel or the opening note in a musical score, you learn that the future of the work is in the present.

ACTION

The structure is simple. You decide ahead of time what variables you will use and for what length of time (see the list below). Variables can be pulled from a hat or called out by the teacher. You stand on stage or off. Someone in the audience has a watch with a second hand. The person with the watch says, "Go," and you begin the exploration. When time is up the timer says, "Time." You sit, and the next person goes, using the same variables and time limit. As the harangues progress, different variables can be chosen by the teacher or pulled from a hat. New time limits can be imposed.

TECHNIQUE

Start with simple limits and short times, from thirty seconds to two minutes. Build up to more complex challenges. For a typical harangue the time limit might be two minutes and the variables might be movement only, no dialogue, and always maintain eye contact with the audience. As the performer begins working he or she should ask, "What do I want to do next? Where in the space do I want to go? What does my back want to do, my pelvis, my feet, my hands? What does my sense of timing say to do next, my sense of dynamics, sense of rhythm? When should I pause? What else can I do; where do I go next?"

When an impulse dies and there is still a minute to go, performers really begin to grow. They run out of ideas and have to search within or outside of themselves for deeper impulses. People do things they have never done before. As in trips, you must find that state of duality: You are totally involved in the moment, while at the same time you are aware of the rules of the exercise, what's been done, and where you are headed. It sometimes helps to have an outside observer call out different variables for the performer. Like peeling away at an onion, the goal is to get to the heart of an impulse. Have patience, try everything, and get around to everyone a few times. You can usually play harangues for several hours in a row.

PITFALLS

One thing harangues bring performers face-to-face with is their own insecurity. There is a tendency to go too quickly, throw away interesting choices, work on nerves alone, pace, or get bored with oneself. A lot of promise gets short-circuited. Side coaching helps performers overcome obstacles. I restructure harangues when a student is flailing by adding or removing obstacles to the exercise. It's a malleable form. Patterns you frequently see are: *sequencing*, in which the actor jumps from topic to topic; *accumulating*, in which an actor builds on one event; *false starts*, when the actor doesn't like the starting point; and *throwing curve balls*, when unexpected elements are tossed in the mix. It's hard to stop a harangue when the performer is doing something fascinating; I leave it up to the timer to decide if he or she will bend that rule. However, if a performer runs dry and still has a minute left, he or she *must* continue. The actor is on, even if he or she sits down, until the time limit is over.

VARIATIONS

Here are a few ideas. There is no right or wrong to this. Let the audience affect you; enjoy the jam-session quality of several harangues in a row.

One-minute monologue, on various topics

Give an open-ended speech.
Tell your life history.
Explain a pet peeve.
Describe what you feel passionately.
Describe what prevents you from being passionate.
Explain why you enjoy being on stage.
Speak authoritatively about something you know nothing of.
Explore a metaphor and amplify it to the nth degree.
Impersonate someone from your past.
Speak about a time when you were most content.

Two minutes, no sound

Explore all the movement dynamics you can.
Always look at the audience.
Keep your back to the audience.
Explore a metaphor and amplify it to the nth degree.
Be nervous, no fourth wall.
Be calm.
Play with the architecture of the space.

Two minutes, verbal and physical

Do an open-ended piece.
Physically portray every sound you can think of.
Start a gesture, accumulate associations, and build to a climax.
Enter and complete one, specific task.
Do five entrances and exits.
Give a "what would you change about the world" monologue.

Do the same monologue in one-word sentences, using large gestures.

Use repetition to get to the core of a statement.

Have difficulty doing something.

Use as much space as possible, moving as little as possible.

Three-minute harangues

Jump from one impulse to the next as quickly as possible.

Start something, stay with one theme, and finish it.

The Law of Threes

Many people will tell you that comedy comes in threes. You do something once, twice, and the third time is the blowoff. I know this is a pattern that works, and I also know there are times when it doesn't. It depends on the context. With some sequences, we intuitively expect a third repetition. Doing it a fourth time would feel excessive. Take for example the last guest leaving a party. You close the door. The guest knocks and says he forgot his hat (#1), then leaves. Ten seconds later he returns for his car keys (#2), then leaves. Almost everyone watching will expect a third interruption. The audience will be disappointed if they don't get knock #3 asking if it's okay to stay a little while longer. The host's anger then serves as a peak to the scene, completing a sequence of threes. A fourth repetition would feel anticlimactic. The phrase is complete and the show moves on. But how do you explain Harpo slipping his leg into someone's hand over and over again? Each time it's so charming, you want to see how often he can get away with it. Conversely, in *Play It Again, Sam*, Woody Allen is at a party where a huge plate of cocaine is being circulated. When it comes to Woody, he unleashes a single sneeze that sends powder flying. Twice would be pointless. It is an action that doesn't fit the law of threes. I decided to experiment with this law to better understand the dynamics of triplets and to recognize how often repetition is called for in a given situation.

ACTION

You choose a simple action to do, like touching your nose. You do the action in patterns of three, using every permutation of success or failure. You vary the pauses, the momentum, and the commitment to the task. You choose the pattern of three actions that feels best, present it to the class, and state each time what you are going to do before doing it.

TECHNIQUE

The action you pick need not be funny. Keep it simple, so that you can do it many different ways. Suppose you try touching your finger to your nose. There are eight possible permutations of successes and failures: s–s–s, f–f–f, s–s–f, s–f–f, f–f–s, f–s–s, f–s–f, s–f–s. Try them all. Success is doing it right, failure might mean touching your mouth instead of your nose. For me, s–f–s with this action feels best. For someone else, f–f–f may work better. This is where your persona differentiates itself from someone else's. When you present the pattern say, "I'm going to touch my finger to my nose," before each action. For some people, touching the nose is matter-of-fact, others are more graceful. For some it's a moment of life and death. Recognizing personal style is a wonderful by-product of these improvisations.

Feedback from the group is important. Ask the people watching to name the pattern. Was it s–s–f or f–f–s? Sometimes people disagree! Then ask if the action has a life beyond triplets, if it is perfect as a triplet, or if it is something that should be done only once? Could you do it five times and still hold their interest? When does the situation peak? This discussion clarifies the need to break a rule to suit the context, the action, and the actor performing.

PITFALLS

The main danger is lack of commitment. Sometimes, nothing feels right. Let's say my action was tying my shoe, which is a very complicated action to begin with, and none of the patterns work. Recognize that this was an action I couldn't commit to. It is what I call a "false action." It's not that I'm a bad performer or that choosing shoes is stupid. Something in my chemistry wants *more* stimulation. To fake interest is deadly, but a basic level of engagement must be found or any action will feel pointless. Don't spend your improvising time trying to find the perfect action. Recognize your mood and what interests you at that moment.

If a script assigned to you *demands* that you be interested in shoes, that's another story. You *have* to find some way of engaging your passions. Does having difficulty with a shoe seem mundane? Why did Beckett use it as the starting action for Estragon in *Waiting for Godot*? A good performer is someone with a healthy imagination who can commit to a range of situations. In these exercises, start with what you love, and work your way out from there. If you like to be elegant, be elegant. Success–failure work can lead to frustration if you don't allow it breadth and play across the full scale of emotional response. Choose an action you want to do. Ultimately, audiences have a great desire for you to find joy in whatever you do.

VARIATIONS

Another way of looking at triplets is to play with the expected and the unexpected. Do e–e–u, e–u–e, and so on. Try it without saying what you are going to do, and see if the audience agrees with your understanding of what is expected or unexpected. You can also make aesthetic choices, like ugly–ugly–graceful. You may be surprised at how the audience perceives you!

- Do permutations with three different actions instead of repeating the same one, e.g., touching my hair, touching my nose, and touching my shoes.

Moments of Glory

If you're going to pay for a performance, you want to see some kind of skill on stage. People like to know that effort has been made for them, that they are witnessing people doing something they couldn't do. Details have been worked out and steps rehearsed, and the audience becomes the final link in the completion of a great piece of work.

This is an exercise for exploring your persona as a consummate master of some skill. In physical comedy, it's important to develop any skill you have—musical, physical, linguistic, etc. Harpo really did play the harp and Chico really did play the piano. Victor Borge couldn't clown around with the piano if he wasn't also an excellent musician. You need to know what it feels like to be a virtuoso, even if you haven't fully mastered an art form. The beauty of it is you need not have great conventional skills as a juggler, dancer, or musician to perform this exercise. It could be something as unconventional as eating marshmallows. Blue Man Group, which is truly a vaudeville act for the nineties, uses paint, junk food, technology, and plastic tubes to create new skills the audience has never seen before, presented with virtuoso flourish.

While you spend nights practicing your musical saw technique, do this simple exercise for presenting skills, even before you are a master. Then try the same exercise with any actual skills that you have.

ACTION

You choose one thing you can do with a little bit of practice. It should have about a 90 percent success rate before you present it. You assume that you are the world's greatest at doing this. You make an entrance, do it, repeat it if it seems appropriate, and exit.

TECHNIQUE

This is an exercise to allow you to see how you function when you are supremely confident. Do not allow yourself to believe you can fail; you are the world's greatest. This can be very liberating for some people. Even if your action is as simple as balancing a stick on your finger or walking with Hershey Kisses in your eyes while whistling, feel how the entrance, the execution, and the completion of the action affects you and the audience. Are you stone-faced from beginning to end? Are you noble, nervous, or exuberant when you are master of a skill? Whatever you discover will add a new dimension to your comic persona.

PITFALLS

A high level of *actual* skill does not guarantee greater response. Introduce real expertise as your skills develop, but remember that juggling nine balls can be less interesting to an audience than three. If the audience smells a desire in you to show off, they may be very grudging to give you their respect. Anchor your art with deep personal commitment and love for the form.

Something wonderful also happens when you present a skill as high art and find that you are a complete failure. This is the moment of the personal clown. If you have the strength to pursue how you deal with that moment of failure, you enter into the world of Chaplin, Eisenberg, Bill Irwin, and other great masters of the art of failure. Dustin Hoffman once said he thinks all actors are really people who know deep inside that someone is going to see they are fakes. Performers willing to recognize this weakness and find joy in it make us all a little bit more glad to be alive.

The "Through the Roof" Lecture

ACTION

You quietly walk up to a lectern and begin a lecture on a topic you know nothing about. Starting at the quietest level of energy, you gradually become more and more engaged, using more space and energy to make your point, until you get completely absorbed and forget whom you were talking to. An outside observer cuts in and signals for you to stop, then you face the audience, take in the reaction to your excesses, and leave without saying anything.

TECHNIQUE

This is a linear escalation exercise. You can only increase in intensity, not decrease. Let's say you are lecturing about the history of clothespins. Start as simply as possible. Gradually begin to illustrate physically what you are saying. As the talk progresses, allow your gestures to become more elaborate. Start to use the entire stage. Reach a launching-off point where you express what you feel so passionately that you become totally absorbed in what you are saying/doing/feeling and forget about the audience. This is when you "break through the roof." Stay at that peak for about thirty seconds before the outside observer whistles, claps, or says something to bring your attention back to the room. Look at the audience, stand still, catch your breath, and without apologizing or speaking, head off stage.

This is one of the most challenging exercises I know. I first learned it from Ronlin Foreman—who learned it from Lecoq—in a clowning workshop. It demands all of the passion and vulnerability a performer has to offer. To reach a peak, it is perfectly all right for the actor to switch topics midstream and start talking about relationships, parents, political beliefs, or anything that sends him or her "over the top." Once the performer reaches the point where his or her passion breaks free of the audience, the actor should not make eye contact again until he or she is caught. A friend of mine, Michael Zerphy, did a sketch that followed this pattern. He played an adult who sees a box of Cheerios, reaches in for the prize, pulls out a plastic plane, and gradually gets totally involved in the fantasy of flying around the room. It ends with him getting caught by his son standing on the table covered in Cheerios. It's the pattern John Belushi used in his Sky Lab Report on *Saturday Night Live* and Gilda Radner used when she played Rosanne Rosanna-Danna giving a news commentary. It's what happens in Chekov's "Harmfulness of Smoking Tobacco" lecture. Try to make the whole journey in about four to five minutes. Start slowly and accelerate toward the end. When done right, it feels cathartic, for both the audience and the performer. Ronlin used to stand next to performers as they "landed" to remind them to breathe, keep their jaw relaxed, open their torso, and receive the audience's shock and delight.

PITFALLS

As you go up the scale, you can't go back down. Do or say anything to break into the stratosphere, but try not to hurt your vocal chords. Yelling isn't the only way to reach a peak; try simply moving more actively, deeply, or passionately. The most deeply involved moment requires that you lose all awareness of the audience. At that point what you are saying or doing must be more important, profound, frightening, or involving than your starting point. Once you break eye contact, never go back to the audience until your reverie is interrupted. When you are caught, say nothing as you drift or slam back to earth. The main reason for doing this is for that marvelous reaction you get when you notice the audience again, the "deer in the headlights" moment of silence. Don't break the spell with apologies or grimaces. Ronlin calls it a "white" moment: Let the angel pass by. Keep eye contact with the audience as you start to exit. Pause, breathe, feel the audience, and exit.

VARIATIONS

Panic and paranoia often appear in this exercise, but quiet, tender, sad, or ecstatic experiences can be explored this way as well. Passion is not necessarily louder and faster; it can be deeper and richer. Play with the soft side of the scale, fully escalating a moment with different colorations. Two or three people going through this exercise in a day is usually enough. It can be as exhausting to watch as it is to do. Use it sparingly. This exercise can also be done in pairs.

Objects and Obstacles

Objects and obstacles turn up constantly in the world of physical comedy. Entire Buster Keaton films were based on struggling with the inanimate. Harpo and Chico Marx often worked together to make the handling of objects impossible for other people. Painting a room, wallpapering, and making beer were classic routines for the Three Stooges. Lucy and Ethel were famous for trying to keep up with a candy assembly line. Quite often these routines were fine-tuned to perfection, with new ideas layered in over a period of years. The Marx Brothers reused routines many times. There are far too many types of objects to discuss each individually. Instead, I'll identify some fundamental principles for exploration. All of the exercises presented here as solos can also be done in duets or groups. It may make sense to do these exercises in the order presented.

Many classic sequences involve building a cascade of actions that are developed one step at a time. Things start simply and get increasingly complicated until they reach a climax. This ends the sequence and sets up the next cascade. We will look at the problems of choosing an object, finding a sequence, and knowing when to end it. A lyrical sequence, such as Emmett Kelly sweeping up a spotlight, creates a fantasy world with its own rules. Consummate performers can bring you into their world and then follow through on their actions with perfect, and often surprising, logic. It's expensive to build a house with a hinged false front that blows over in a hurricane with a window on the second floor that fits over your body, as Keaton did in *Steamboat Bill Jr.*, but it was a brilliant ending to an increasingly complex chain of events.

This can be tricky work. It's hard to know what to do first and how it should end. Dealing with objects requires a substantial amount of rehearsal and rigging. You have to have a point of view and something to say. Some things can't be done in a classroom. Other things are best rehearsed in pantomime. Start with small, simple objects, develop a vocabulary, and go from there.

The First Obstacle

ACTION

You stand on a cube or a chair with no moving parts. You assume it is difficult to get down. You try to step to the floor and fail. You try it a few different ways until you succeed.

TECHNIQUE

See how many different actions you have for getting down and how many ways you might fail. Do you have vertigo? Are your legs too short? Do you enjoy the height and regret leaving the summit? Commit to each choice and explore it to its limit before moving on. Stand on your right leg and reach towards the floor with the toes of your left foot. Go up to the "edge" of that action, where your toes are barely one millimeter from the floor. Milk the last possible millimeter, moving forward into the action. Let your whole body register the "yearning." If you actually touch the floor, the game is over and you have won. Celebrate, acknowledge your victory, and move on. If you fail, pause. Let your failure register, and move on to the next tactic. When you deal with objects, these concepts of going *forward* in the action, *milking* the millimeters, coming up for *air*, and *celebrating* your victories are key. Your pursuit is rich because the audience enjoys seeing complex means to a simple end. It makes them feel both superior and empathic. When you solve a problem, your victory must equal emotionally the volume of the failure leading up to it (back to Newton's laws).

A person of average intelligence and coordination has no problem stepping down to the floor. But in the world of physical comedy, the action of stepping down can be a matter of life and death. The possibilities are limited only by your imagination. If you believe in your dilemma, the audience will too. Find something to believe in. Open your horizon to the audience whenever possible. Your battle becomes private if you don't allow the audience into the struggle. Seek complicity. Focus out on the start of an action, look out in the middle of failure, focus out when planning your next step. It's a habit that helps your work resonate, even when playing in fourth-wall situations. It gives your work breadth and lets people see who you are.

Objects on Stage

After exploring an obstacle, put it in an environment. See the object in relation to space. This is similar to the exercise on takes with a five dollar bill, only now you enter the space with a profound relationship to your environment. It's not a person on the street finding money, it's an actor alone on stage with an object. Begin by encountering the cube.

ACTION

You place the chair or cube center stage. You enter from the wing with the intention of crossing the stage. You then encounter the object, deal with it, and exit.

TECHNIQUE

You can deal with it in one move or take several steps. Treat it as an obstacle or step right over it. Don't worry about plot or motivation. Why did the performer cross the stage? To get to the other side. Who put it there? Who cares. Leap on it, crawl under it, come running back and trip over it. The possibilities are only limited by your imagination. You can create a life-and-death dilemma or an elegant dance routine. Play with pauses, eye contact, milking your actions, and all of the dynamics listed in the previous exercise. This is a way of sneaking up on your persona. Actors engaging the cube unconsciously strengthen their presence on stage because they are entering the space with a point of focus. The object provides opposition; the exercise gives you something to be *interested* in. The focus helps you lose self-consciousness, and persona arrives.

PITFALLS

Be true to your point of view. Whatever you start with, commit to it so that your next step comes from one point of reference. If you see it as a threat, don't waiver from that opinion until you or it does something to change your mind. The easiest way to screw up is to take false steps that don't interest you. Be logical. Any point of view is better than none. If you can't find a journey that interests you, change the speed of approach, your level of energy, or any variable that may surprise you into a sequence of vital reactions.

VARIATIONS

Here are some possible approaches.

- Try seeing it for the first time.
- Try being afraid of it.
- Try treating it as a dance partner or something you love to play with.
- Try pretending it's not there.
- Try a whole sequence maintaining eye contact with the audience.

Prop Rounds

ACTION

Everyone brings an object to class. Each person plays with his or her object individually for a few minutes, looking for tricks, sounds, balance points, and hidden qualities. Then the class gets into small groups. They sit in a semicircle, put one object in the center, and do a series of go-arounds, or rounds. One person gets up, does something with the object, and sits back down. With no critiquing, someone else gets up and does something different. You go around many times, until you feel like you have exhausted all possibilities, then go around a few more times. You move on to another object, until everyone's object has been used.

TECHNIQUE

Choose a simple object. Get familiar with its weight. Do a motion study with it. How heavy is it? Where is its center of gravity? Can it be tossed, balanced, rolled, bounced, or opened? Look for voices it may have. Any moving parts? Any transformative possibilities—can it be used as something else? Jonathan Winters and Robin Williams are masters at this. You may dance, sing, talk, attack, or cajole the object. When you break into groups, see what the other five or six people do with your object. It need not be a logical or narrative use; you're just tossing out half-baked ideas. Keep things moving; don't spend more than fifteen to thirty seconds per person per round.

PITFALLS

Keep breathing and opening up to the audience while presenting your ideas, or you will feel claustrophobic.

VARIATIONS

- Once every object has been played with, go off alone for fifteen minutes and choreograph a short piece with a beginning, middle, and end using your object. You may incorporate any of the images you saw in the brainstorming session, or simply explore one idea that interests you. Bring your studies back to the whole group and show them to each other. Get feedback on what moments were most clear and most interesting, what needs more development, what went on too long, and what would be the best payoff. What was the audience hoping you would do next?
- It's also fun to see what you can find at tag sales, craft shops, and plastic supply stores.

Imaginary Objects

Pantomiming objects is a good way to practice two important techniques: pauses and moments of surprise. A moment of surprise is that sudden, unexpected change in the usual course of events. With pantomime, you can practice spilling water, breaking an expensive vase, or poking yourself with a stick in the eye without actually causing any damage. This allows you to develop some wild situations. You can practice with the real thing later on and see what works better. Some things are better left to the imagination, as with Marcel Marceau, and sometimes it's better to build everything, as with Blue Man Group.

ACTION

You mime a simple action such as brushing your teeth, lighting a cigarette, or sewing on a button. You see how many minute steps it takes to accomplish the action. Each step is an opportunity for a moment of surprise. The possibilities begin the moment you enter. How many ways can your task be interrupted before succeeding?

TECHNIQUE

Each interruption is a moment of surprise. *Pause* after each surprise to let your reaction sink in and the next step to develop. Solutions can surprise you as well. In performance, you would not want to show every single step to an audience; you would pick and choose the best ones. For now, work slowly and deliberately. Repeat actions to get them right. For the sake of training, it is important to learn to take your time and explore all possibilities. Choose and arrange the surprises you like best into a sequence with a payoff, and present your study to the class. Try doing an action that has at least three interruptions, surprises, and pauses.

PITFALLS

Do not affect a persona. Character emerges as a result of your pursuit of the task. It is *important* to keep your horizon open to the audience every twenty seconds or so, so that you don't smother in a private world. Your actions must resonate in space, just as an actor's voice must fill the auditorium. Beginners often get engrossed in their actions, and it becomes a private problem.

VARIATIONS

Pantomime a duet action with a partner, such as painting a fence, and mark every interruption and surprise with a pause. Build a cascade of actions between the two of you. Keep an eye on each other, so that you know whether you have been splashed or helped. Laurel and Hardy often work this way with real props.

Difficulty with Objects

This exercises your ability to struggle with an object's true function. Anytime you've had trouble opening an aspirin bottle, you've done this exercise. Anytime you try to accomplish something with a prop or an object, you enter the realm of difficulty with objects. The trick is to make the dilemma feel real. In *Godot*, one obstacle is putting on a shoe. In the hands of Beckett, the dilemma is profound. The English comedian George Carl is a master at mishandling clothes, microphones, and his own body. Avner Eisenberg can find five minutes of hilarious business in simply trying to light a cigarette. I saw a brilliant routine by a Russian clown once. He took ten minutes to set up a chair; that was the whole routine.

ACTION

You choose an object that has a function and try to use it. You explore ways to fail at your task until a solution presents itself.

TECHNIQUE

Find the object's low-end actions and high-end actions. If you were hungry and had a shrink-wrapped sandwich, the low-end actions might be looking at it from all angles or trying to find a loose place in the plastic with a finger or with your teeth. High-end actions would be squeezing it in a vice, cutting it with a saw, or having someone else come by and open it easily. Start with the low end and move to the high. If a brilliant solution presents itself, make note of it and put it toward the end. Pursue your objective relentlessly. Follow each action to its limit. Engage the whole body more delicately, more thoughtfully, or more desperately—whatever is appropriate. At the end of one tactic, pause and try another. Come up for air with the audience. Arrange your discoveries in a sequence and present them. Keep the best and throw out the rest. Start simply and save the most imaginary solutions for the end.

PITFALLS

The hardest thing to develop is an order. It's a very intuitive process, and you may be the worst judge of what to keep and what to throw out. Let the audience decide. It's easy to overlook a step or play with too many actions at once. Over time you become adept at recognizing "good" mistakes that lead you down the path of richest dilemma. Repeat an action only if it builds the suspense. Be careful not to succeed at something you meant to fail at. Opening the sandwich on the first attempt will suddenly blow the entire piece. Part of rehearsing is to find how much pressure, weight, and leverage are needed to do a thing the *wrong* way. You need not lower your intelligence or adopt an artificial character. If you are graceful, use grace; if you're aggressive, attack it. Find endings or let endings find you. Lecoq says the clown fails at what he intends and succeeds at what he does not intend. The solution often comes from something that was done earlier, preferably something the audience has forgotten about. Let moments reverberate. An ideal sequence has a pleasing, internal logic. Each step builds on previous steps to move forward dynamically. Use the steps you have taken to create an aesthetically complete universe.

VARIATIONS

It's *very* helpful to place a successful move in the middle of your struggle. It's the change-up that gives the audience hope. Find an interesting transformation, turn the object into a puppet, or balance it on your nose; use any kind of magical event that allows your imagination breadth. Now place the breather in the failure sequence and repeat it. Which moves interest you now? How many failing tactics should you use before you succeed? When do you digress? How do you celebrate success? Slow take, stone-faced, or exuberant? Should the whole piece be a celebration? Learn to pace yourself. Vary your choices: Use sudden moves, suspended actions, delicacy, or clumsiness.

Here are some classic routines to experiment with that are all based on difficulty with objects.

- Bring a folding chair on stage and try to open it up.
- Try setting up a microphone stand.
- Set up a reclining beach chair.
- Look for directions on a map and try to fold it back up.
- Make a cake from scratch.
- Set a dinner table.

Scenarios with Objects

Full-fledged performance pieces grow very easily out of combining object rounds, object studies, moments of surprise, and difficulty with objects. All of the former rules apply: advance the play, find variations, stay open to the audience, use the beginning to find the end, find small victories that let your piece breathe. Doing solo work with obstacles also prepares you for partner work. In comedy teams, often the partner *is* the obstacle, as in Monty Python's argument sketch. Exploring the dilemma of a pun with a partner could lead to an Abbott and Costello "Who's on First" routine.

ACTION

You choose an object, and present movement studies, difficulty studies, and brainstorms to the class. You use feedback from the audience to pick and choose the elements most worth developing. You return a day later with music, costumes, and other actors if need be. You present the piece, get feedback, and do one more round of development if necessary.

TECHNIQUE

Watch everything the actor does, and discuss what of the things he or she did was most interesting. What had the most promise? Ask these questions: Should this be a difficult struggle or a subtle character study? Should there be music? Does it feel like a silent piece or a verbal piece? Is it a virtuoso demonstration of cool moves or a lyrical piece? Or a disaster? Is it realistic, absurd, or a dance piece? Help the actor decide what to work on for the next class. The performer should pick a style that makes the most sense, and be true to that frame. On the next day, the actor should make an entrance that lets the audience know what the frame is: going on a date, late for work, looking for peace of mind, here to entertain, in an absurd universe, etc. The performer should let the audience see the situation. The object can be in the space already or it can be brought in.

Learning to give good feedback is as important as learning to write material. Actors are sensitive; always start by mentioning the things that worked, even if it was only 5 percent of the whole. Use that 5 percent as the basis for further exploration. You may stumble on a great routine, or you might come up empty. If you do, throw it away and start the process over with a new object, but always find something to mention before abandoning an idea. What object might work better?

PITFALLS

I like to have people pick something that is not too breakable or expensive. A portable cassette player will most likely get destroyed in a high-end choice. Beware of glass or other sharp objects. Avoid endings that destroy your object, unless you're willing to buy a new one for each performance and rehearsal. *Never* throw or break anything that could injure someone in the audience. Frustration as a character can rapidly turn into frustration as an actor. Give yourself room to breathe and succeed as you go along—it will help you find steps. Find the joy, the nobility in your actions.

Once you have developed a good scene, play with all the steps in the sequence. Make sure they are necessary and add detail where needed. Look at it from the top, the bottom, and from the inside out. Listen to your audience; see if you are missing any beats. Is anything dragging on too long? Rearrange the order, if need be. Keep your actions clear and take your time. Vary the dynamics. Vaudevillians spent years developing the same ten minutes of material in hundreds of performances. Don't be afraid of the obvious—sometimes you need to embrace clichés. Don't prolong a scenario forever. End it when a solution presents itself; you may find a step that opens the next path.

Summary

This chapter is longer than others because so many solo exercises are also done with partners or in groups. These are the buttons, the exclamations, and the building blocks of basic comic business. It is by no means a complete set of exercises—you may need to invent your own.

To review:

- Actions are determined by context.
- No move is worth risking an injury.
- Advance the play one step at a time.
- Go forward to the last millimeter possible.
- Open yourself to the audience's horizon.
- Don't grab for high-end solutions first, unless it's a one-step blackout.
- Use the steps that have gone before to advance the play.
- Succeed occasionally, to let your dilemmas breathe.
- Use pauses for clarity.
- Let the ending find you when you least suspect it.
- Acknowledge your victories.
- Remember the motor: where were you going, how hungry were you, etc.

The more an action is needed for the survival of a character, the better it will work. Small actions take the most skill to play; large actions need the most relaxation.

····3·Duets

All of the exercises in this chapter are done with a partner. For the sake of clarity, I will refer to the actors as A and B. When doing partner work, it's a good idea to trade roles in any exercise, even if it's as simple as letting A start first one time, then repeating the exercise with B starting. Exercises in this chapter include Ping-Pong, artillery, duet improvisations, servant-master relationships, and working with scripts.

Ping-Pong, the Basic Interaction

ACTION

Actor A and actor B stand on opposite sides of the stage, then walk toward each other as if to pass like strangers on a street (or actors on a stage). One pauses, the other reacts, then pauses, and this continues with A and B reacting and pausing one person at a time. After about a minute of acting and reacting, the exchange, or volley, ends.

TECHNIQUE

Think of this as a physical form of Ping-Pong or tennis: You are tossing impulses back and forth. A makes an action, B responds, A answers B's response, and so on. This is the supreme exercise for staying present and in the moment with someone else on stage. It has many levels of complexity, but on the simplest level you respond spontaneously to the actions of your partner with an action of your own. It is *essential* that you end each phrase. Your action could be long, short, close, or far away, but it must end clearly so that your partner can respond. Don't think about the response; just move and pause. Wait for your partner to end his or her phrase and remember to keep breathing. One reason for doing this is to train actors to move with clarity and specificity, even when there is no "plot." You can physically contact your partner, build a train of thought, or change dynamics completely. React the moment your partner stops, so that your action is not labored or psychological. Hit "the ball" back and forth, high and low, fast and slow.

PITFALLS

Move impulsively, get ahead of your sensors, and react viscerally (short of hurting your partner!). One common mistake is to pause to decide how you should react. It's too late. One would never do this in an actual tennis match; just go. Don't worry if you repeat yourself or feel like it's too small or brief a reaction. Stronger reflexes will develop. Trade partners and notice how patterns change with other people: You get more aggressive, more playful, more mysterious, or more silly with different partners. This exercise tries to evoke an awareness in real time of this chemical interaction between two living, breathing performers. It is the essence of acting. A complex, psychological moment between two characters on stage is lifeless, regardless of the language being used, if the actors are not actively or instinctively volleying for position on stage through real reactions in each performance.

Beware of habitual reactions that are not responses to your partner. Begin the exercise with these questions: How does that person make me feel? What do they make me do? Do I move closer or farther away? Can I yield as often as I lead? See everything. Your partner's vitality, spirit, and presence is the motor for your actions and vice versa. You should know something about each other after playing Ping-Pong that you didn't know before.

Don't limit your actions. Agree ahead of time to suspend ordinary rules of social behavior. Actors must be willing to take emotional, physical, and spatial risks that they wouldn't take with strangers. Break up dead-end patterns, what Lecoq calls "pyramid" architecture in an improv. Aggressive stand-offs of yes–no–yes–no have nowhere to go. Miming a story of "Don't I know you? Ah yes!" is dead from the beginning, because the ending is already written and the two players become victims of a predetermined set of actions, unless something unexpected happens to jolt them into truer reactions to each other. This exercise should be done without sound before moving on to verbal variations. It is the purest way to play. Do not substitute pantomime language for real reactions.

Variations

- Add sound to the reactions. Begin by using open sounds, grunts, sighs, and noises rather than articulated words.
- After a few rounds of Ping-Pong, partners usually want to move at the same time. Remove the pauses; take the brakes off the action. You can still pause if you choose to, but feel free to move together. The improvisation should still be driven by reacting to each other. As pairs become more active, play with distance, traveling, physical contact, yielding to partner impulses, and ultimately, using language.
- Change partners midimprov. With a room full of partners playing Ping-Pong, it naturally develops that partnerships will play off each other. Partners may be exchanged and new impulses followed. Trios can be formed, solos can be left to move on their own, or two pairs may become a quartet. When in doubt, pause; see the world and move on.
- Go back to back; use shifts in pressure and weight with no eye contact.
- Play Ping-Pong with the small end of the scale, using just head, neck, and face muscles
- Play on the smallest scale possible, using just breath and the tiniest of reactions to a partner's eyes. This variation helps students listen more closely to subtle, internal shifts and be aware of the power of a tiny gesture or action.
- Use Ping-Pong as a warm-up between any two people who have scenes together in a scripted show.

Slaps and Kicks: The Slap

Action

Partner A stands side by side with partner B, facing the audience. Partner A takes a straight-arm swing across his or her body and smacks partner B on the mouth. Partner B turns and looks at A, faces back out, and then winds up with his or her inside leg and kicks partner A in the rear.

TECHNIQUE

The slap is a noncontact slap; the kick makes real contact. Both moves rely on a huge wind-up to imply a large force being delivered. First the slap: A sets up a wide swing with his or her outside arm, leaning out on the outside leg so that the whole audience sees how much force will be delivered. A extends the arm with fingers held flat together, and takes a tiny pause right before swinging. As A swings, he or she should keep the body facing front and use the shoulder socket to help stop the momentum. *Do not* turn your body toward your partner—it makes it too easy to really hit him or her. The "slapper" must stop the swing a good six inches away from the mouth of the "slappee." Measure the distance a few times, swing slowly, and then gradually increase the speed, making sure you are always able to punctuate the move without actually touching the slappee. The person being slapped has the hands loose in front of him or her, and claps to make the sound, or "knap," just as he or she appears to be hit. B's head snaps straight back and reacts. The whole action is counted in three steps: (1) eye contact between partners to say, "ready," (2) face front and wind up, (3) swing and clap and react.

PITFALLS

Partners needs to practice the timing of the wind-up and follow through so that the sound happens exactly when the slap occurs. It's very easy to put too much tension into the slapping arm, as well as into the arms of the clapper. B must not telegraph that he or she is about to be hit. B should remain calm as A winds up, keep his or her hands and arms long and loose, and clap and snap the head at the exact moment of impact. This requires practice. It is easy for the slapper to reach too high or too low on the swing, and lose the illusion of smacking the other person in the mouth. Be consistent and deliberate with the swing, making a clean pause with A's hand in front of B's mouth, and don't be too quick to move it away. Give your partner time to recover. Finish reacting to one slap before doing another.

- Trade off. A hits B, B hits A; A hits, A hits again; or A tries to hit while B ducks and smacks A after A does a full, 360-degree spin from the previous swing.
- There are several other kinds of slaps, from full contact to elegant fakes. Another simple slap is the V slap, in which A stands at a ninety degree angle to B, raises his or her hand above the head, and pulls it down and up in a rapid V motion with a punctuation mark at the beginning and end of the V. Partner B claps and reacts at the moment of impact. The slapper always misses the slappee by a few inches.
- Avner Eisenberg once taught me a nice technique for clarity. Right after A slaps B, separate B's reaction into three steps. Make a distinct pause on each move:
  1. Touch the slapped cheek.
  2. Turn to look at A.
  3. React.
- Try these three steps in a different order and see how it feels.

Slaps and Kicks: The Kick

ACTION

Actor A kicks B in the butt.

TECHNIQUE

The classic, Charlie Chaplin kick in the butt (he is a masterful kicker!) is as much in the upper body as it is in the foot. Keep in mind, silent film comedians went for broke in the old days, in a roughhouse manner that would shock modern audiences. You can still get quite a good effect without all the pain they endured. The kick is delivered with a hop-step. If A is kicking with the right leg, B is on A's right. A steps out behind B on the ball of the right foot and pushes his or her weight in a quick hop back onto the left leg. In jazz dance terms, it's called a "ball change." As the right leg goes out for the wind-up, the arms are cocked in unison down low and twisted with the torso to the left so that the whole body is wound up for the kick. As A's leg swings through, the arms and shoulders twist in opposition to balance the move, giving the appearance of a great force being delivered to B. Your foot must land flat, with the inside of your ankle lengthwise along the fleshy part of your partner's butt. The energy should be held, so that no serious force actually goes into your partner. It does, however, shock the person when done properly. If you kick with your left leg, your partner stands to the left.

PITFALLS

It takes a little practice to find the right angle for your foot to land. You need to be almost perpendicular to your partner for your kick to work. Watch out for poking your partner with your toe, hitting too low and bruising his or her legs, or putting too much force into the kick and hurting his or her back. If your partner gets shoved forward, that's far more force than is necessary. Put the force into the wind-up and follow through with the arms and torso, but don't let it carry over into how hard you kick. Talk with your partner to see how much force is too much. The blow should glance up, not into, your partner's butt.

VARIATIONS

Put a hat lightly on your partner's head, so that when you kick him or her, the hat goes flying (your partner can help it to fly by tossing his or her head as part of the reaction to being kicked). You can also kick someone standing next to you with the reverse side of your ankle. Instead of opening out away from your partner and using the instep to kick, stay close, flick your ankle up "backward," and tilt your knee down, a backhand tap landing lengthwise on the butt with the outside edge of your foot instead of the instep.

Developing a Slapstick Routine

ACTION

Two actors stand side by side; each is wearing a hat. An inciting action—a slap, cough, kick, bow, etc.—makes one of the hats fall. Both partners go through a series of steps to try to get back to where they began.

TECHNIQUE

This is an excellent exercise for developing comic logic. Every time a step is made, two or three new steps become visible. Which do you choose? Should you hit B back, should you offer to pick B's hat up, should B do nothing until you kick him or her again? Trust your intuition, try something, move on to the next step, and see if you can choreograph a six- or seven-move sequence where each step feels right. Talk to your partner, change steps, make sure you are both happy with the progression, and then rehearse it so you can repeat each step smoothly and present it to the audience. If everything works except for the next-to-last step, you may have to go back through and change everything else to make it work. Audiences watching will instinctively know when the partnership is "working"—they will enjoy your routine. Harder to pinpoint is when the logic breaks down or you make a false choice. Go one step at a time and make sure it all pays off.

This is the essence of comic timing. Some sequences are only four moves long, and then the phrase should end. Learn to recognize whether it is a blackout or the beginning of a full-length piece. Add to this hats, kicks, canes, coats, or other objects, and you can have quite a complex routine. Again, rather than aim for a specific style or character, do what feels natural. If you slap someone and feel bad, make that guide your next step. Apologize. Do something nice; it will create new opportunities. If you enjoy slapping someone, and the slappee gets mad, that will guide your choreography down a different path.

PITFALLS

It's so easy to get off track. The first step may lead logically to the second, but the third step might end up being a red herring that defeats the whole piece. All of these exercises require lots of trial and error. Have different partners demonstrate their routines as they develop. Give them feedback. Watching other partnerships can help actors see where his or her path lies. If you're malicious, go for it, but be consistent. The decision to suddenly do something nice won't work unless you buy it, and it still may not be what the audience wants. You can usually pause a routine at any time and ask the audience what should happen next. Nine times out of ten, people will agree on the same step. It may be hard to articulate why, but most people know what feels right. The audience has basic human expectations and an innate sense of justice that determines whether a piece will succeed or fail. You also need to execute all kicks, trips, slaps, and other moves with a fairly high degree of skill. A missed step is like a sour note in a song and can undermine a perfectly well-written routine.

VARIATIONS

Sometimes, even though all the moves are well executed, a whole piece fails because it just wasn't what the actors wanted to do to each other. I've seen carefully rehearsed, well-executed pieces get no response, because the actions were somehow foreign to the participants. Make it your own piece by recognizing your inner urges. For the kinder souls in class who dislike violence, try a whole sequence with yielding actions motivated by kindness rather than anger. See what that provokes.

A general warning on slapstick comedy: If slaps, trips, smacks, and falls are put into a piece purely to get a laugh, as is the case sometimes with the Three Stooges, the less likely the business will have any lasting impact (pardon the pun). The more an action is needed within a scenario for the characters to survive, the richer the comedy. I saw Disney's *Beauty and the Beast*, which has quite a bit of slapstick humor in it. The action between Gaston and Lefou is pure knockabout master-servant, which is well executed, but after the first smack in the face, the other slaps seemed redundant and garnered only mild chuckles. The biggest laugh came not with Lefou getting hit, but with the Beast taking forever to say "please" while wooing Belle. It was more integral to the plot. Too much slapstick tends to nullify itself.

Also, comic business can fall flat if the actions aren't pursued. If actors never deal with the physical and emotional repercussions, the audience doesn't care about the action. The Marx Brothers, on the other hand, garnered laughter and applause for their use of slapstick by always having a sense of joy underlying their anarchy, especially when taking on pretentious people. They understood and fully embraced the absurdity of the human condition, which again goes back to actions necessary for survival. Their love for playing together always showed. In *Play It Again Sam*, Woody Allen tipped his hat to them for giving his life meaning. Wandering in despair into a movie theater, he finds the will to live by watching the Marx Brothers hit each other over the head. Nice use of context.

Artillery

Before creating full-fledged relationships on stage, sharpen up interpersonal skills that are frequently called on. These are the partnering instincts actors need to develop a dilemma to its fullest. These skills often blend together, but it is useful to focus on each skill individually when training a performer's reflexes.

Matching

ACTION

A is on stage; B is in the wings. A is the receiver. B instigates an entrance with a specific level of energy. A instantly matches it, they sustain it for twenty seconds, and then exit. Trade off, with B receiving and A instigating, or go around the room adding a new person each time in the wing as instigator and the previous instigator becoming the receiver.

TECHNIQUE

This is a very simple game designed to make sure a receiver is sensitive to a partner. It's a controlled form of Ping-Pong. The easiest way to see if it is a match is to pause the duet and ask the audience if A is higher, lower, or just right. It is also an exercise in sustaining an energy level for at least thirty seconds. If B comes in with a high energy choice, A must match and maintain the level B started with so that he or she doesn't drag the energy down or lift it higher. This can produce very realistic scenes; for example, a person comes in very sad and upset, and the partner consoles him or her. It can also be quite absurd, with neither partner knowing what he or she is doing, while staying in the same energy zone. When in doubt, A should just mirror what B brings in. In advanced variations, richer counterpoints can be encouraged.

PITFALLS

Make sure the instigator makes a strong, clear start—low or high energy, happy or sad—or it all turns to mush. Sometimes a person comes in with a high energy choice, jumping up and down over winning a lottery, and the partner's enthusiasm is slow to catch on. This flattens out B's joy and blows the exercise. Actor A *must* find a way to instantly overcome his or her reserve and respond in a way that matches, but is neither higher nor lower than, B's joy. Beware the selfish receiver who says, "I didn't feel anything from my partner." It's your job as an actor to *validate* the instigator's choice, not to quibble with it. Once all partners are sensitive to this, advanced variations can come into play.

VARIATIONS

Matching really just means that you are joining the frame established by your partner without question. The way you respond can be more complex than just mirroring.

- Try the counterresponse. Your partner comes in crying, and rather than cry with or console him or her, you find it all rather funny and start giggling. The trick is to make sure you respond exactly to B's specific choice. Listen closely; react for real. The counterresponse can still maintain B's state and not take it higher or lower. This produces great counterbalance dynamics, like Eeyore and Piglet or Norton and Kramden.

- Do the unexpected. With more advanced players, you can delay the correct response or counterresponse. The principles of Newton's laws of motion still apply, but laughter erupts when the skillful player can use responses that create great, knowing imbalances that take advantage of the audience's desire for justice and equanimity. If you play an imbalance well, you can build up an audience's expectations and create some wonderful explosions. If you wait too long to equalize a situation, you lose the audience, and the piece collapses. Like a slingshot, if you stretch a piece too far, it will break.

- Skillful players can change each other's level of energy. Do a variant of this exercise in which the players start at one place, shift up or down the scale of dynamics, and both respond. Do several transitions without leaving the stage and find an ending.

Interruptions

ACTION

A chooses a solo activity that requires concentration and B interrupts it in as many ways possible.

TECHNIQUE

The skill is to develop an eye for the exact right moment to interrupt. Vary the kind of interruption, so that A never finishes what he or she was doing. It is best to start at the low end of the scale and work up to the high. For instance, A might be concentrating on a difficult chess problem. A high-end interruption would be knocking the board over. Save such extreme choice for later on, so that you can find all the delicate interactions first. Many an improv leads to a dead-end fight if you're not careful.

B should start with simple actions, like standing too close to the chess board or dusting the furniture and trying not to be noisy. Partner A can help B by providing clear opportunities, what I call "floating moments," for the partner to puncture. Use all available tactics for artillery: Play verbally, silently, emotionally, and psychologically. Try helpful actions when disrupting actions begin to run out of steam. Like difficulty with objects, it's important for you to let your partner and the audience catch their breath and think peace is restored in order to set up the next wave of interruptions. When an ending presents itself, take it, finish that round, and change roles. Don't be surprised if after completing a round, a whole new set of actions appear that begin a new game.

PITFALLS

For an arrow to land, the target must be receptive. It is much more interesting if the low-end offers the interrupting partner makes have some kind of effect on the person trying to concentrate. A can be nice about being interrupted or fly off the handle. Sometimes this game never works because nothing actor B does will rattle actor A, which turns it into a different game, namely, "How do I get my partner to respond to me?" This is never a very interesting game. The activity must not be so private or so precious that the audience doesn't enjoy seeing it be interrupted. If the interrupter appears too mean-spirited, the action quickly loses appeal. B must be as sensitive to A's wish not to be disturbed as A is to being disturbed.

VARIATIONS

This game works well with groups. When played with three or more actors, the goal can be for B to drive everyone from the room. By combining interruptions with the next exercise, escalations, you can produce classic situations such as:

- an audience watching a movie while someone eats popcorn too noisily
- a restaurant or waiting room where one person has the hiccups
- a classroom exam with one person making noise, sharpening pencils, and causing a distraction

Will Smith played this game in the movie *Men in Black* while taking a competency test. An English troupe, the Moving Picture Mime Show, did a wonderful version of this game in white larval masks. One person can be interrupted by several, or a whole group can react as a chorus to one person. There is a classic vaudeville routine called hellzapoppin' in which someone never finishes what he or she sets out to do because of constantly escalating interruptions. The best duet version of this game I've seen was played by a pair of Italian theater clowns called Les Columbianos. One person was trying to recite Omelet (Hamlet), while the other used some remarkably simple interruptions to totally derail the partner's efforts. Practice interrupting a single partner to gain a foundation for escalating larger situations with more people.

Escalations

The ability to take steps in a solo, duet, or ensemble piece that build on all previous steps is essential for actors. When practicing escalations, the low end of the scale is as important as the high end. The most creative choices are often on the low end, where performers have more room to maneuver, breathe, and think. Many people rush the early steps and go for the bigger fireworks immediately. As you go up any scale, things tend to go faster, you get more tense, and there are fewer options. At the top of the scale, stay below the level of tension at which all control is lost, actors get hurt, audiences plug their ears, and all qualities turn to chaos.

Start with linear escalations. Each step must build the tension, not dilute it. Go from the smallest, quietest actions up the scale to the largest, loudest actions. For example, a child trying to get a mother's attention would start the scale by saying, "Mom?" a few times and some gentle skirt tugs before turning purple by holding his or her breath. Notice that in this case, the "loudest" action is in fact silent. A simple solo escalation, like counting to ten, reveals how much tempo, volume, emphasis, and proper awareness of previous steps produce dramatic tension. Linear does not mean evenly paced. If you were going to threaten someone by counting to ten, the way you vary emphasis and silence between numbers is what makes the suspense grow. Put the climax at ten, not six.

Once you master the dynamics of linear escalations, vary the rules. The tiniest step near the top of a scale is sometimes the best pay-off. The last moment before an explosion is often silent. Vary the steps from verbal to physical back to verbal, then add a surprise ending. Try risking the cliché and do exactly what the audience expects, but go further than anyone has gone before, such as Buster Keaton's brilliant chase scene with enormous boulders in *Seven Chances*. You can't believe he'll go any further, and then he does. Eat the piece of paper, take your clothes off, or pour the whole bottle down your pants. As long as no one gets hurt, it may be the only way to end the escalation.

ACTION

Actors get in pairs with an object that is unbreakable, e.g., a towel, a piece of aluminum foil, or a plastic water bottle, and A does something that will surprise B without hurting him or her. A does it to him- or herself, the audience, or B. A gets them to react, then decides what the next action should be. The actors use space. A surprises B three or four times in a row. They trade off, and B surprises A. They go back and forth surprising and reacting to each other. They keep their faces as simple as possible. They can try cooperation, curiosity, aggression, one-upping, love, intrigue, or envy. They pick and choose an order that builds and present it to class.

TECHNIQUE

Don't start with writing. Just try stuff. Brainstorm, go back and forth, and pay attention to what buttons you can push on your partner. You can repeat actions, but make sure you are both conscious of previous steps. You can do actions together, back and forth, or play teacher-student with one person learning from the other. The actions often have silly, scatological, sexual, or absurdist overtones. Use space, surprise attacks, language, emotional setups, or whatever it takes to create an escalating situation. Ask what actions get the ball rolling and what actions are "toppers." Choose one direction; decide how you would enter, what should happen early on, and what is the payoff; and escalate to that peak. Finish that train of thought before trying a new sequence.

The brilliant comic often leaves a little bit undigested that the audience forgets about and pulls it out at the end of a sequence as a final button, a cherry on top of the sundae. See if there is anything you can add to the payoff that was introduced early on. Rehearse the whole sequence and eliminate extraneous moves before showing it to the class. Escalating scenarios include falling in love during a golf lesson (object: the club), a clerk trying to fit a jacket on a customer (object: the jacket), or Laurel and Hardy moving a piano up an insanely long set of stairs (object: the piano). Switch partners and see how different people play.

PITFALLS

Stay away from narrative objects, like dolls, joke vomit, or other props that have unyielding identities. The simpler the better. Actors need room for transformations, surprises, and manipulations. A person putting on a sweatshirt may start with it as a shirt, but in the middle of the difficulty have it turn into an uncontrollable monster or a head-dress. Plastic vomit will always and forever be plastic vomit. There are many paths toward a complete buildup of effect, and you need to find the chemistry between you and your partner with the object as a catalyst. Henri Bergson calls it a buildup of minute cause into gigantic effect. Avoid antagonistic relationships by trying cooperation or misunderstanding instead.

VARIATIONS

There are many exercises for escalations. Objects are good for starters because actors have something concrete to focus on. It shows how many possibilities are hidden in a prop and why Chaplin would do a hundred takes of the same scene with countless variations. It's a little like that game in elementary school where you take a word like *encyclopedia* and see how many other words are hidden within it.

With objects

- Use two similar objects, with each partner having his or her own hammer, bottle, etc.
- Use two different objects, one for each partner.
- Create an escalation with a series of objects taken out of a bag or sack.
- Think of an escalating scenario first, then find props and choreograph the scene.

Without objects

- Count from one to ten with a partner and make it interesting. Try it five times in a row and still make it interesting.
- Tell a story that rhymes, alternating lines.
- Insult each other.
- Try sleeping in the same room with one person snoring.
- Write an improvised song-and-dance number from scratch. A makes the smallest noise or movement he or she can. B responds with the tiniest bit more interest, energy, or volume. To-

gether, build a melody and choreograph instant dance steps. Go until A and B end up in a full, Broadway-style song-and-dance number. It's the gusto that counts—no points taken off for strange lyrics.

- Watch videos of classic routines. Note the type of steps and the variety of logic used by comic masters. Lucy and Ethel's food fights, Groucho and Harpo's mimed mirror frame, and many other masterful escalating situations can be found on film. When you see an escalation on video, pause it halfway through the build and try to predict what the actors will do next. Advance the play, see if you were right, and see how they surprised you.

Answers

Whenever a question is posed in an improvisation, any answer is better than none, unless indecision is a conscious choice meant to move the situation forward. It's always more interesting to see *Lorene* go to the *graveyard* for a *spoon* than it is for *her* to go to the *place* to get some *stuff*. "Sitting on the fence" is a common habit that muddies the water. It's as easy to be vague physically as it is verbally. Do a verbal round of answers and follow it immediately with a physical round.

Verbal Version

ACTION

A is an interviewer asking B, who is an expert in some field, all about B's career and the challenges facing him or her. B is not told ahead of time what the area of expertise will be.

TECHNIQUE

Like any expert being interviewed, you are allowed to think, pause, have mannerisms, and not know every answer, but in general assume you are a leading authority and have passionate views about the subject. A needs to ask difficult as well as simple questions. If A becomes suspicious of B's answers, or senses B is stalling or being evasive, A should zero in on those doubts and ask piercing questions that reveal B's innermost thoughts. Good questioning is as important as finding answers. Keep playing physically and notice any opportunities for Ping-Pong, sitting/standing, or other rhythmic games. Catch every sigh, cough, glance, and head turn and use it.

PITFALLS

Don't try to pick a topic that sounds funny or embarrassing, for example, best nose picker, greatest mass murderer, or you will have a one-laugh exercise that is fruitless. The skill should be specific, and B should supply answers that build on the interviewer's line of questioning. Listen to each other and stay engaged emotionally. A brilliant improvisation can turn into a brilliantly scripted scene, if you can record it.

VARIATIONS

Think of a scene in which one person needs to know something from the other. Play the whole situation with partner B consciously supplying answers, then trade, *until you are both adept at it.* Monty Python's dead parrot sketch is a perfect example of having answers. An everyday occurrence turns into a hilarious battle of logic and stubbornness when a customer wanting a refund confronts a shop owner who sold him a dead parrot. The performers investigate every logical and illogical angle to the conflict, leaving us laughing and satisfied with an absurd exploration of all three of Newton's laws. It's like watching a great tennis match. The Monty Python actors had a great flair for pursuing arguments. The argument sketch and the cheese shop sketch are great examples.

Also try:

- asking for directions
- getting help at a shop counter
- portraying a cop pulling someone over for reckless driving

Nonverbal Version

ACTION

A and B find an imaginary or a real line on the floor. They both stand on it at opposite ends of the room and approach each other on a collision course. They assume it is a silent universe. They find a way to pass each other.

TECHNIQUE

Partners can go around each other, over, under, face off, get pushed off, or do an elegant Ginger Rogers–Fred Astaire exchange. What's important is that the game of Ping-Pong requires real tactical questions and answers that are made physically. Unlike the verbal interviewer situation, partners lead and follow at the same time in silence, with no designated leader.

PITFALLS

Beware of pantomiming dialogue. In the rich world of physical play, an improvisation won't sound silent if the actors accept a level of existence that is pre- or postlanguage (more Blue Man Group than Marcel Marceau). Assume your actions take place in a universe that needs no spoken language. When you try to spell something out that is easier said than done, you might as well just say it and limit the work to a more pedestrian zone.

VARIATIONS

- Pretend the whole space is divided into an imaginary grid, like a tick-tack-toe board. Do a two-person improv in which you travel through the space on the board using straight lines with ninety degree turns. This creates opportunities for parallel, perpendicular, and collision courses. Allow moments of play to develop.
- Do the same grid and allow dialogue when needed.

Endings

ACTION

Actors A and B put two chairs side by side and pretend they form a window ledge on the fortieth floor of a skyscraper. A stands on the ledge, B is a stranger who sees A. They find an ending in one minute.

TECHNIQUE

The solution can be verbal, physical, mundane, or absurd, but you *must* find an ending. Other time limits can be imposed, but the goal of the exercise is to get actors in the habit of completing phrases. Often, ending a phrase opens up new opportunities. Practice ending one phrase and beginning another that also ends in one minute. See how much distance you can cover in five minutes of improvising. This helps train actors to undo logjams. You don't always need brilliant blowoffs, you just need things to end so that you can move on. Moments of genius are few and far between; any ending is better than sitting on the fence. The craft of comedy requires many commonplace solutions before brilliant ones arise.

PITFALLS

Extreme situations are chosen because they have such clear choices for endings. Starting in crisis allows actors to get to the point without wallowing in exposition. Even so, people will still do their best to avoid an ending. Actors love to ditz around in an improvisation. As much as they can be consumed with stage fright, they will let situations drag on ad nauseam. Trapped in dialogue like "Open the door," "No, you open it," "No, I think you should," actors will often bat the responsibility back and forth because neither actor wants to take a risk and decide what's behind the door. Meanwhile, the audience is screaming on the inside for you to make a choice and open the goddamned door! It goes back to the answers exercise. These are natural instincts that need to be worked through. If you have the courage to call something an ending, it will become one.

Working on a scripted show where the endings are already written doesn't solve the problem for you. You *must* play as if you don't know what will happen next. You need to *justify* the thought process beneath the words. Make them your own. Comic actors must know their instrument. The actor who makes intelligent choices about the pitch, speed, intensity, and justification of his or her actions will be far ahead of the actor who believes the script does it for him or her. Actors must *earn* the brilliant text and games that the playwright has written.

A great actor uses a script like a major league ballplayer uses a bat and ball—with a 110 percent focus and drive and an ability to adapt to instantly changing patterns. A mediocre actor holds the bat out like a stick and lets the text bounce off it with no real personal engagement. Going through the motions is the worst kind of theater, and tacking phony comic blocking on top of it is equally painful to watch. Professional repertory actors are as guilty of this as untrained amateurs, if not more so.

VARIATIONS

Try one-minute endings as a spelling bee. Write a number of crisis situations on index cards, put two actors on the stage, and pick a card. Give the actors one minute to find a logical and satisfying end. Call time if they don't finish in one minute and have two new actors try it until you can go around the room and any two actors can end any situation in one minute. Keep the work urgent. Try the same exercise with two- or three-minute time limits, so that actors develop a sense of how long some choices take to play out. Try

- a man proposing to a woman
- a person trying to sneak past a maitre d' in a restaurant
- a doctor examining a patient
- two people in a rowboat that springs a leak

Duet Relationships

Unless it's a solo show, almost every comedy is built on colliding relationships, introduced a pair at a time. Working with partners is the essential unit upon which all ensemble complications are based. Whether it's straight man to clown, salesman to customer, or husband to wife, good comedy requires actors with an openness to the opportunities found in each other. These exercises create character and relationship through reactions found during play. When someone reacts to you it defines that person's character, which in turn defines your character. The action in a script or scenario may appear obvious to you, but the logic, clarity, and timing is always a shared responsibility between actors.

If an exercise doesn't seem to work, admit it, try to figure out what isn't working, and fix it. All these exercises require a little tweaking from time to time to stay on course. There is a fine line between a sublime, honest improvisation and a confusing mess. Common errors with many of these duets are:

> You're working too fast.
> You're pushing for an artificial result.
> You have too many themes on your plate at one time.
> You aren't really paying attention to your partner.
> Your dynamic range is shallow.
> You've decided whom you think you are before experiencing anything.
> You have bad chemistry—you didn't start out respecting each other.

Begin in a spirit of teamwork. Respect each other's strengths and weaknesses. Physical life is crucial, no matter how verbal you get.

Hutte's Points

This is an exercise passed on to me from a workshop by Swiss clown Garde Hutte. I don't know where she trained, or if she invented the exercise, but I call it Hutte's points. At its core, it is an exercise for eliminating ambiguity by always having a clear focus on either the space, the audience, or another performer. It's very good for teaching students specificity and disciplined choices. It also demonstrates how easily actions can create plot, character, and relationship without having to think of funny things to do.

The order is hard to remember, so have an outside person call it out for a few rounds, then let people do it on their own once they've learned the sequence. There is nothing sacred about the sequence; you may try other patterns. It's the discipline of specificity that is important. However, it's interesting to note that with Hutte's sequence, the performer checks in with the audience before doing an action, which is often the case with clown work.

ACTION

Two people face the audience, eyes closed. The first to open his or her eyes and look at the other is A, the second is B. A does a sequence of actions while B watches. At the end of the sequence, B does the same sequence, using different points of focus. The following steps are done standing still, except for step 4:

1. Look at the audience.
2. Look at a point in the room (beside your partner's eyes, since that is the next step).
3. Look at your partner.
4. Look at your point again and travel to it (or do an action related to the point).
5. Look at the audience when you get there (or complete the action).
6. Look at your partner.

This ends one round. Your partner now answers your sequence in the same order: audience, point, partner, action, audience, and partner. This goes on for several rounds, until the relationship reaches an ending phrase.

TECHNIQUE

Start simply and neutrally, with no preconceived battle plan. In step 2, don't let your eyes drift around the room ambiguously. Be definite. The first thing you look at becomes the point. It can be on the floor, the ceiling, or anywhere else, as long as it's not your partner's eyes. Have an outside person call out each step. Start slowly and methodically so that you can get familiar with the pattern. Gradually pick up the pace until you can do a whole sequence very quickly, in ten seconds or less. Once both partners have the right steps in order, let them go on their own so they can vary the pauses, distance, speed, etc. Do each action clearly. The main variable is the point of focus chosen and the duration of each action. If both partners keep focusing on the same point, a fight might develop. If you move the point around the space, themes of revenge, one-upping, intrigue, or budding friendship will develop spontaneously.

Pitfalls

As you get further into the exercise, it's easy to confuse the order of the steps. Don't. When you complete your action going to the point (step 4), it is very tempting to look at your partner for a reaction. You *must* look at the audience first, which keeps the event public, then look at your partner to see what he or she will do next. It is also tempting after step 1 to look at your partner before looking at the point of focus. Don't, unless you want your partner's body to be the point. Feel free to use physical contact as themes develop. You may get in positions where it is next to impossible to look at your partner; do your best to try. Don't feel like you have to be frozen when your partner takes a turn. You can and should keep an eye on the other player, without distracting yourself, so that you know when your sequence begins. The event you create will then be driven by reacting to each other.

Variations

As always, try pairing up with different people, and notice how the rhythms and themes differ. It can be a bit confusing, but you can do this exercise with three people. Add a third round for player C, in which C has a choice of looking at A or B. I find this less rewarding for training purposes.

We Can't Talk Here

This deceptively simple game is a great way to get actors physically engaged while using text. It is excellent preparation for playing comedies by Shakespeare, Moliere, and Feydeau, and leads easily into classic situations of servant-master, straight man-comic, etc.

Action

Two people stand near each other. One says to the other, "We can't talk here." The other reacts. The situation builds until they find an ending.

TECHNIQUE

It begins as soon as one person enters the space. A is the motor (the one who speaks first), but both partners are responsible for developing the themes. Once the game has begun, continue until an ending presents itself. If antagonism runs dry, try cooperation. If both partners hit a wall of frustration and can do nothing else with each other, convert the game—apologize, cry, hurt someone, or pull out a new card that allows the relationship to continue to develop. Some people can play in silence with absolute integrity for four to five minutes, others jump right to highly verbal exchanges.

Urge actors to use space, tempo, and body language—not just dialogue—to communicate. Engaging physically gives everyone more rage, curiosity, desperation, or bonhomie to react to. On one level, you are creating a dialogue. But the observant partnership gets the most mileage out of reacting to actions and body language as well. Countless games develop, and the observant team can play out each volley that comes up before changing the game. Counter each other's gestures, take an exchange down to the floor, create an exit, and pursue all phrases to completion.

PITFALLS

One of the biggest dead ends is insisting on answering the question. The exercise works best if you focus on *how* its played, not *why*. If A says, "because the teacher told us not to talk," the playing options get limited early on. Assume that the actor who says, "We can't talk here," means it. Use repetition and vocal color to create interaction. B can accept the premise or disagree, but the value of the interplay is in feeling your effect on each other. Play more politely with this partner, more violently with this partner, more inquisitively with this partner. As an actor's instincts surface, you begin to see what kind of player you are. Sometimes you need a spark to ignite the relationship. State your feelings, thoughts, and concerns with real physical commitment. Invest a lot of energy. If neither person accepts the premise that it is *very important* not to talk right now, you can generate very little excitement.

Many times, a partnership runs out of steam after a few minutes. End it. Trade roles, have the other person be the provocateur, and see how the games change. Switch partners, get around to five or six different people, and see how many other levels of play there are. If you always do and say the same thing, you aren't really working off of other people, you're trying to force the same game on everyone. That gets tiresome. Good practice for type A personalities in class is to do the whole exercise as responders, not initiators. Let the other person always lead, then respond.

The Servant-Master Relationship: Delivering a Letter

This is one of the most enduring relationships in theater, from Aristophanes to the present. Servants and masters appear in Moliere, Shakespeare, Balinese shadow plays, French farce, sitcoms, and countless plays, films, and television shows. It is a relationship rich with opportunities for movement and improvisation. It demands high stakes, strong needs, and great intellectual and emotional resources. The relationship can be base or mythic, popular or heroic. I use a simple situation to help students connect to the roles: a master asking a servant to deliver a letter.

ACTION

Two actors decide who is the servant and who is the master. The servant leaves the stage. The master folds a piece of paper to act as a letter, calls the servant in, and orders him or her to deliver it.

TECHNIQUE

This improvisation could be over in ten seconds or it could take ten minutes. It's all about looking for opportunities. The givens are: the servant must desire to serve, and the master must need the letter delivered. This need is the motor; every dilemma has one. Call the servant "Servant," the master "Master" when speaking to each other. Catch and react to every nod, move, wiggle, or innuendo your partner makes. You could try to plan on being a kind master or a haughty servant, but the relationship soon grows into rich, uncharted territory as soon as you just react to your partner's actions. *Do not* predetermine characteristics such as who is smarter, meaner, or wiser. Let the relationship develop through interaction. Find out what kind of a master your partner *makes*, and what kind of a servant he or she *makes*.

Servants should look for opportunities for surprises and digressions, but always try to serve the master. Masters should look for opportunities to see their servants as lazy, disobedient, illiterate, or as confidantes, but always have a strong need for the letter to be delivered. Use pauses for clarity. Complete your phrases. Find and exploit escalations, interruptions, Ping-Pong, and other variations as needed. Move forward when a card has been played out; end sequences when the time is right. One-minute scenes can be as satisfying as ten-minute scenes, it just depends on the degree of engagement, the wit, the emotional risk, the physical momentum, and the honesty and imagination of the players.

PITFALLS

When your partner doesn't see an opportunity for a game, move on. It's hard to read minds, and this exercise can stall out when one player insists on pushing a premise the other player isn't interested in or fails to see. Get fully involved by physically manifesting your psychology—it's the only way for your partner to tell what you are thinking. This gives you each more to react to and throws more fuel on the fire.

VARIATIONS

Change roles. Find out what you do in each role, regardless of how you might cast yourself. Try the exercise with other partners and see how your inclination to be kinder or meaner, smarter or slower changes based on instinctively reacting to different people. Maybe they are bigger or faster than you; this will force you to change tactics. Chemistry with a new person affects your instincts, so respond to the actor you are playing opposite. This is *essential*—it is where truth lies.

- Find a scripted letter scene and play it with your partner using the text. Letter scenes can be found in Shakespeare, Molière, Stoppard, Restoration comedies, and others.

- Cast yourself in a scene against type and find a way to tap your natural instincts. Try taking a personal trait and playing its counterpoint. If you are an actor who normally speaks loudly, try speaking softly. There is that side in you, whether you exercise it or not. If you have great intelligence and wit, try using it to play a person who is dense and slow.

- Once you have played both roles, with script and without, try other servant-master situations. Try master berating servant, servant tricking master, master and servant on a quest, servant saving master's life, master meets master, and servant meets servant. Look through scripts and novels for examples of servant-master conflict. Put the dialogue aside at first, improvise the situation, then go back to the text. Keep it simple. This will help you to connect to a role. Don't be misled by stereotypes; the same words can be used by a bully or a coward. Work with your partner to see what chemistry exists between you. You don't have to understand why something works when it does, just develop an instinct for where the life exists with your partner, the dialogue, and the space.

The roles of servant and master also prepare you for other contrasts, such as:

- smart-dumb
- tall-short
- fat-skinny
- slow-fast
- brave-cowardly
- honest-dishonest

Should you find yourself cast in one of these archetypal relationships, personalize your role. There are as many versions of Sancho Panza and Don Quixote as there are actors. Work honestly and nobly. Allow for trial and error. Laurel and Hardy worked a long time to develop a rich relationship. The Smothers Brothers, Lucy and Ethel, Abbot and Costello, Kramden and Norton, and Burns and Allen spent years exploiting their differences. They complemented each other *and* maintained their individuality. There are some great role models out there; study them. Partner work may not suit you, but most actors at some point must play off another actor as if their lives depended on it. On stage, it does. The expression "We died out there" captures a very real feeling, as does "We killed them."

Impersonations

This exercise is similar to solo impersonations, explained in Chapter 2, only this time you work with a partner and present a classic duet routine. Choose roles and learn verbatim a Harpo–Chico, Lucy–Ethel, Sid Ceasar–Imogene Coca, or other duet routine, present it to the class, and then teach everyone some of the phrases. The same variations and pitfalls apply.

Working with Scripts

Servant-master work taps many skills: listening, seeing, Ping-Pong, rhythms, interruptions, escalations, answers, and vocal and physical color. Apply these same skills to other relationships. Find a two-person scene in any comedy. Look at Moliere, Shakespeare, Feydeau, Kaufman and Hart, Beckett, Peter Barnes, Stoppard, or Ionesco. Practice your skill at identifying the games going on in the scene. In commedia, these are called the *lazzi*—comic business that may digress from, or be a primary factor in, the development of the plot. It might be a game of insults, a flirtation, a game of interruptions, or any of hundreds of other games that people have played since time immemorial. A good comic actor recognizes the games being played underneath or alongside the text and finds actions that bring it to life. Spontaneous timing combined with a deep awareness of the other players, the audience, and the author's intentions can breathe life into a comedy.

ACTION

Actors A and B choose a duet scene from a scripted comedy, present it to the class, and have classmates identify all the potential games hidden in the text: rhythmic, spatial, one-upping, etc. The performers then improvise each game suggested, using their own actions and dialogue. Once they are off-book, they try each game using the text. What games fit A and B? Which ones serve the play best? How many games are needed to bring the scene to life? Is it one essential game or several combined? A and B go through the script and choreograph the actions according to the games they have chosen. They present the scene the next day with full text, props, and costumes.

TECHNIQUE

Never stop playing actively with your partner. What levels do you click on? What is the primary game? Every scene has many interpretations, and you should play with several before blocking the text. Look closely at the script and decide where events peak. When does a new round begin? Is it a steady build or a cat and mouse game? Do you need props or pantomime? In physical comedy, it is usually better to have the real thing. Develop an eye for the structure of the event. See where more rehearsal is needed once you present it to class. Is there a phrase you never solved? Is there a place that needs another half-hour choreography rehearsal? Is there an exchange where the attack or the rhythm doesn't feel right? Does the audience see something you are missing? If you are playing Cyrano and Roxanne, the romantic language alone won't save you. The primary motor is that Cyrano is madly in love and Roxanne doesn't know it. Everything you do will be dead in the water if that essential passion is missing.

PITFALLS

Some people play better in their own words, others must have a script. Do both. It exercises different parts of your brain. Make sure the games you explore are supported in the text. Avoid going on automatic once you block a scene—it is deadly. The choices you discover must be rediscovered *every time*. Comedy takes a lot of energy. Surprises must be just that. Even respected equity theaters often fail to keep a comedy alive because the actors don't keep working the *play*. This can be due to a lack of rehearsal, a lack of training, or a lazy habit of letting the language do all the work. Games must be played in real time or the performance becomes a virtual comedy, with faux laughter. Use your imagination every night. Use the script as a road map and an integral part of, but not a substitute for, the entire arsenal brought to bear on every struggle faced on stage. Handling something as witty as Tom Stoppard or Oscar Wilde poses the extra challenge of finding that rare actor who can transcend rote memorization and actually be that bright, witty, and aphoristic in his or her imagination. Don't take the author's genius for granted.

VARIATIONS

Do the opening coin toss sequence in *Rozencrantz and Guildenstern Are Dead*. Recognize what variations are possible and try each choice. Is one character bored and the other frustrated? Try it. Does one person insist on flipping coins to prove the other wrong? Try it. Are they just really good friends who find these kind of games intriguing? Try it. Does one need the other's counsel and advice in order to survive? Try it. All choices are based on context, so both of you need to read and discuss the play. Decide what you think the show is about. Some choices are quite serious; don't be afraid of the deep end of the pool. In *Rozencrantz and Guildenstern*, the stakes are life and death.

Why do they play with each other in the first place? Find an important reason. Is this a new game or one they have been playing all day? Those are two very different setups. Do they both wish they could break the pattern? Is one glad that the other is trapped? Work to make each choice believable. This is your job as an actor, and vital choices will then surface. Use your own instincts, tap into resources you didn't know you had, but always react truthfully to your partner. Do you and your partner have an instinct for who fits which role best? Use it. Use trial and error with the audience to discover which version works best. Whatever you do, don't try to be funny or profound. Just do your job.

Your chemistry and insight will produce either a boring show, a nasty show, a silly show, a confusing show, or a brilliant show. This is true with any play you work on. My point is, if you take on *Rozencrantz and Guildenstern*, spend a good deal of time tossing coins and philosophizing, to see how *you* play those games and why. Learn to work with linguistic, existential, mathematical, and physical variations, before blocking the show—literally.

Summary

Here are frequent phrases I often use with partner work: Comedy floats, tragedy sinks. Spin up, not down. Choose a strong motor you can commit to. Don't bite off more than you can chew. Finish what's on your plate. Play one card at a time. Let the moment ripple, let the ripple return, react accordingly. Let the reaction point you to your next action. A hollow motor makes for false play. Remember your original motor. Any ending is an ending if you say it is an ending. Use pauses. Recognize transitions. When in doubt do the obvious and see where it leads. Do something because your partner makes you, not because you have a clever idea. Don't be afraid to end an improv. Use interruptions. Leave at the wrong/right time. Float a balloon for your partner to puncture. Recognize the game. Layer in new phrases to routines you have mastered. Do the expected. Do the unexpected. Change dynamics when you're tired of each other. Do something kinetic for a change of pace: juggle, play music, sing, or dance.

....4 . Trios

Working with a partner develops basic comic muscles. As soon as you add a third person, a more delicate sense of play is needed. It becomes less about you and more about ensemble. Trios prepare you for ensemble work: They teach you to be generous. Escalations, interruptions, difficulty with objects, and obstacles, all are doable, but the dynamics change. No individual makes up more than a third of the actions. In the best groups, each individual personality always comes through, though no one individual is doing too much or too little to assert him- or herself. Everyone sees what his or her job is and fulfills it. The more you all focus on a unison action, the more your individuality will surface. The more you all *try* to stand out from the others, the more you will all look the same. Trios are fascinating to watch because the center of gravity is always in flux; all three must juggle in order to achieve equilibrium. Exercises in this chapter include the bench, the expected/unexpected, and various trio improvisations.

The Bench

This is a purifying exercise that helps strip away nervousness, impatience, and mugging. It teaches students an awareness of the themes and variations found in simply seeing and reacting to each other. It helps actors develop an open, available presence. Instructors at the Lecoq school use it to teach actors the tactical psychology of silent play.

Every time I introduce the bench to a new group of students, I remind them that for this exercise *they* are funny, their *ideas* are not. It has many traps into which beginners often fall. It is about allowing yourself to just *be* on a bench and interact with other actors. Play in silence. Be patient. Often nothing interesting happens for the first minute or two. In a way, it's similar to the dynamic of three strangers standing together in an elevator who unconsciously move at the same time or shift because of the person next to them. Seen from the outside, these actions are full of meaning ripe for development by a knowledgeable actor. Keith Johnstone calls it "the kinesthetic dance." Actors should freely explore the possibilities of this dance much further than real strangers would actually do in public. The audience will find that watching three unique personalities interact honestly and spontaneously can be very entertaining, even with no plot or dialogue.

ACTION

Three people stand in the wing. There is a bench, or three chairs side by side on stage. Actor A enters and sits. Actor B looks for the right time to enter and also sits. Actor C looks for the right moment to enter and sits. All three actors act and react to one another's presence. After a few minutes they stop, and a new group goes.

TECHNIQUE

The first person goes out on stage and sits. This is like the first pebble being thrown in a pond. There is no plot, no bus to catch, no lost love waiting to arrive, no lunatic looking for a victim, just an open actor entering and sitting on a bench. Don't try to make a comic entrance. When the ripple settles from that action, the second actor enters. There is a time that is too soon and a time that is too late; practice will tell you when the moment is ripe. Once B sits, A and B react to each other. Avoid grimaces or faces that erase the building tensions such as phony smiles, perfunctory waves, handshakes, and so on. Pursue the tensions that are there further than you would in real life. Go where it is most interesting. When in doubt, just look at each other, longer than you would in reality, and be present to what you feel. Then look out at the audience. Notice everything. Where are the other person's hands and feet? Is he or she breathing or not? Should you move closer or further away? When the time is right, C enters. Now all three people must act, react, and pause, based on what the other two people make them do. Themes will begin to develop. Some groups are more antsy than others, some get giggly, some are very sad. All groups can produce rich studies in human nature, if their actions are true. Use an outside coach to stop the exercise and get people to start over whenever someone pushes too hard to make a plot, bring on a character, or provoke a situation artificially. What they have right in front of them—their own personas—is far more interesting.

PITFALLS

Keep your faces as simple as possible and explore the mystery of whom each person is. Don't duck out of the tensions or release them with a phony smile. Have an outside guide point out false grimaces when he or she sees them. Don't be afraid of stillness. All three people looking in one direction can be fascinating. People will cross their legs unconsciously at just the right moment. A hand shifts exactly when a foot wiggles. Audiences watching can see good listening when it happens. Suddenly, lovely little gestures, head turns, and moments of surprise occur that are so complex they look choreographed. To get there, you need to take your time. Opinions will vary on what is a right move and what is phony, but you've got to start somewhere. Gestures such as glancing at a wristwatch or holding a hand out indicating rain are in the category of what Lecoq calls "parasitic" gestures—habitual responses that should be avoided at all costs during this exercise. Picking at a fingernail with feigned interest is too private an action and will drive you into your head.

For the bench to work, all three must keep their peripheral vision open. Sit up and breathe so other people can see you. Remember to notice what the third person is doing, especially when you're avoiding him or her. There are plenty of options as the exercise progresses. Actions will develop, and games like two-on-one or monkey-in-the-middle will pop up. Roles will reverse. Something usually gets the ball rolling. If you are too cautious, nothing will happen. The main problem is usually the opposite: too many people trying to force things to happen. Be patient. When tensions develop, pursue them.

VARIATIONS

The bench can also be done with five or more people. The chairs can be rearranged to set up different tensions. Try creating your own pattern of chairs in the space and see how the games change. Other variations are mentioned in Chapter 5, under scales.

Alone–Company–Crowd

When my theater company adapted the *Krazy Kat* comic strip for the stage, we explored one strip in particular that seemed to capture George Herriman's unique world. It is basically a variation on a bench scene and a wonderful structure for experimenting with head turns, silence, dialogue, entrances, and exits.

ACTION

A mouse enters, sits on a log, and says, "Alone." A cat enters, sits on the log, and the mouse says, "Company." A dog enters, sits on the log, and the mouse says, "Crowd," gets up, and leaves. For your purposes, you need not worry about playing a cat, a mouse, or a dog; just be three actors—A, B, and C—entering and sitting on a bench or on the floor.

TECHNIQUE

Start with an empty stage, all actors in the wings. A enters, sits, and looks for the right moment to say "alone." B then looks for the right moment to enter and sit next to A. A looks for the right moment to say "company," and so on. The exercise ends when A leaves the stage and B and C react. Stay with the same roles and repeat the exercise a few times, playing with simple variables. Try entering, sitting, and looking straight out; turning to look at each person as he or she enters; or having the person playing A change the length of the pauses. See what feels right, then trade roles and see how the timing shifts with the new chemistry. The value of this simple world is that each variable stands out clearly and people watching can really appreciate how subtle choices have hugely different impacts.

PITFALLS

Be deliberate: Make sure you can repeat all actions and timing exactly. It's easy to move too much, gesture unconsciously, move vaguely, or forget what you did. Discuss what you will do out loud before trying it. This exercise calls for precision each time. You are looking for the exact right time, the exact right phrasing, the exact right person to play actor A, B, and C.

VARIATIONS

An additional bit of dialogue can be added after the mouse exits, so that the other two actors each have a line. When the mouse exits, the dog says, "Funny little person, that mouse," and the cat answers, "Yez, and sometimes a bit kweee" (queer). Again, try it with takes to each other, with no eye contact, with takes on the exit, after the exit, stone-faced, etc. Use the audience as a sounding board, try three different versions, and see if you agree on which pattern works best. You may not.

The Expected

ACTION

A makes a strong entrance, B enters in the way that would be most expected based on what A did, C enters and does what is expected based on A's and B's actions. Continue the pattern going A–B–C for a few rounds, then trade leaders.

TECHNIQUE

Before getting too carried away with surprising an audience with the unexpected, it is a good idea to make sure you can first do what is expected. If A enters and puts his or her left arm out, B should enter, stand next to A, and put his or her left arm out. C then enters, stands next to B, and puts his or her left arm out. The action need not always be a mirror; if A says hello, B can say hello a third above that, and C then must say hello a third above that to create a full chord. If there is debate about what is expected, try to think in musical terms of melody, harmony, and rhythm, call and response, and again, Newton's three laws. The point is to take no unexpected curves. It's always tempting to be the clown, to do the wrong action on purpose, to try to stand out. Develop a strong understanding of what is logical first before introducing the unexpected. As Lecoq says, you must first learn to be a tree, a tree that is just a tree, before being an angry tree, a tree in a hurricane, and so on.

PITFALLS

It can get boring. Before you add surprises, see if you can first find expected patterns that break the mirroring mold. Use progressions, decaying actions, long–longer–longest, or rhythmic games that follow the rules of what is expected.

VARIATIONS

As each phrase ends, A, B, or C can start the next one, or they can do a reverse sequence of C–B–A, A–B–C, and C–B–A. Agree ahead of time which variation you are going to do, or it can get very confusing.

The Unexpected

ACTION

This exercise starts the same as the expected, except at step 3, C does something unexpected. The actors pause, make eye contact between all three, fix it, and end the phrase. A does another action. B does the expected, and again, C does something surprising. They keep the pattern A–B–C, so that C is always the one doing something unexpected. They find an ending.

TECHNIQUE

Unexpected actions can be interpreted broadly. It can be the same action with the wrong timing or a surprising action with the right timing. C can notice the mistake, or he or she can blithely continue as if everything were all right—it depends on the chemistry of the group and the individuals involved. The ensemble can escalate the failure or solve it quickly, but an ending must be found. Ping-Pong and an awareness of one another helps this exercise. When in doubt, look at one another. Solve the problem by changing roles or positions or finding an answer. Give everyone a chance to be the end person, the middle, and the starter.

PITFALLS

Getting frustrated with the person who is doing the unexpected can lead to the group getting frustrated with the exercise. Use all the variables found in difficulty with an object and succeed–succeed–fail to keep the piece moving forward. When a pattern of succeed–succeed–fail gets frustrating, break it by doing something right. Celebrate your victory. Have someone else unexpected be the person who screws up. Come up for air frequently to the audience, to keep the piece from getting too private or claustrophobic. Don't drag it out too long.

VARIATIONS

Choreograph a trio that has at least four unexpected phrases in it before finding a solution. Present it to the class. Get feedback, throw out what doesn't work, and develop a new piece. Leave the rules behind if you need to. Quite often, an exercise must be dumped because it is less interesting than the raw material you stumble upon.

Slap Trios

See Chapter 3 for stage slaps.

ACTION

Three people stand near each other. One person slaps another, somebody responds, and several slaps later the piece ends.

TECHNIQUE

Use any noncontact slaps, swipes across the face, or backhand double slaps. The first time out, each group should write a five-step sequence. Rehearse each step, and make the fifth step resolve the situation. Anyone can slap in any order. Try to follow the logic that feels right. Some moves can get quite complex, with partner C ducking as partner A winds up, and partner B getting caught on the wind-up. That all counts as one step. Go back to step 1 and rehearse up to where you left off to feel what is the right next step.

PITFALLS

The sound has to be sharp, or the slap feels phony. The angles to the audience need to be rehearsed, so that the illusion of being slapped is complete. The inner feelings of the performers need to drive the action. If you don't feel like slapping someone, don't.

VARIATIONS

Add hats, coats, a dinner table, and food, and turn it into a food fight that can be carefully replayed, step by step, with each move thought out and rehearsed.

Hats, Coats, and Canes

This is the same exercise as the duet slapstick routine, with more people and props. It is also an advanced variation on the slap trios. Work through the logic of each step, practice the execution so that you can do it well at least 90 percent of the time, and then present your piece to the audience to see what else needs to be done. Develop your skills in trios with these props, and you should be able to move on to larger groups and other props. In *Noises Off*, it's sardines, clothes, and furniture. In *Scapino*, it's plates, cups, and food that require masterful choreography.

ACTION

Three actors enter the space and stand side by side wearing a hat, a coat, and carrying a cane. An inciting action dislodges one object and the actors pursue a cascade of actions to get back to where they began.

TECHNIQUE

The technique is the same as with slapstick duets. Because there are three people, more complex patterns emerge. One person can duck just as another reaches, while the third becomes an unsuspecting victim. Trios by their nature also can form aesthetically pleasing patterns. Rather than play the whole exercise as a series of missteps, try choreographing unison gestures; it can be just as fascinating.

PITFALLS

These are the same as with slapstick duets.

VARIATIONS

Use the same props, and try expected, unexpected, escalations, or interruptions. Use fewer props. Try having two hats, two canes, two coats, or one of each, between three people, and end up with one person getting all the objects.

Nosy Neighbor

ACTION

A has something very important he or she needs to tell B in private. C interrupts.

TECHNIQUE

This is a three-person version of interruptions that also escalates. Give A and B high stakes, such as a marriage proposal or asking for a first kiss. C can be a stranger, a brother, a parent, or whatever makes the most sense. Look for the right moment for C to enter. A and B should float setups, or great moments that C can puncture. Play with entrances and exits; milk the millimeters of all actions. In *You Can't Take It with You*, Tony and Alice are about to to kiss when the mother interrupts. As soon as the mother leaves, the sister interrupts, then the handyman, the grandfather, the maid, and so on. It's a version of this kind of hellzapoppin', only C is the only interrupter or is someone who just doesn't know when to quit.

PITFALLS

It helps if the audience knows what A wants to tell B and where they are. Do some kind of minimal setup so that the audience enjoys the interruptions without confusion. Decide if you are outdoors or indoors. Watch out for scenes that are intrinsically tragic. Confessing that "I ran over your dog" or "Your mother died" is a usable motor with high stakes, but it calls for skillful actors comfortable with black humor. Decide what the frame of the scene is—realistic, absurd, or a fairy tale. Commit to it, or the event makes no sense.

The Scale of Desire

ACTION

Two actors are on stage. A third person enters downstage of them, unaware of their presence. The two upstage actors (A and B) find a tremendous desire to approach C. They escalate the approach in incremental steps, building to as high a level of suspense as possible before C sees them. They find an ending.

TECHNIQUE

The desire to approach C can be to steal, to attack, or plain physical attraction. A and B could build up to the moment of meeting C, A and B could be thieves sneaking up on C, or they could be warning C. *Don't* preplan the scenario! A and B just look at C, look at each other, and the Ping-Pong begins. Feel what pulls you toward C. Play without dialogue, or C will turn around and see you. When C catches A and B, the exercise transforms. Now A and B must run for the exit, explain themselves, or start a new game.

PITFALLS

C needs to suspend a certain amount of disbelief and limit peripheral vision, or the game is over before it begins. C can help a lot by ignoring little noises behind him or her. Listen for the right moment to move, sit, stand, or walk in a circle, and float A and B some opportunities. Use ESP! C is as much a part of the build as A and B are.

Once you develop a scenario, repeat it and add dialogue. A and B can do asides that C pretends not to hear. Add music; choreograph the best moments. Rather than ending the exercise once C discovers A and B, play it out and pursue the scenario that develops after the moment of discovery. Add dialogue for C if needed.

Make Us Laugh

ACTION

Trios of actors have fifteen minutes to plan something that will make the audience laugh. They come back together and each group presents their piece.

TECHNIQUE

This is one of the crueler exercises in theater, but it does provoke interesting work and healthy discussions. Whenever actors *try* to be funny they usually fail, because trying to be funny and being funny are two different things. Audiences resent being asked to decide if something is funny, and digging for laughs often carries that danger. We usually laugh at people involved in a task or a dilemma. Their focus keeps the work relaxed, instead of desperately seeking approval. Do something without worrying about the laugh quotient, see how it goes, and discuss it afterwards. It's always interesting to see what people come up with. Actors often stumble onto melodrama, romance, psychodrama, and theater of the absurd instead of laughter. This is a good exercise for stimulating an exploration of theater styles.

PITFALLS

The audience must endeavor to remain fresh for each piece, as a true audience would. Wipe the slate clean between each act. Don't let the audience intentionally resist laughing; it's not that kind of exercise. It's hard enough if you are the last group to go after six groups in a row.

Take a break to stay fresh. Be neither supportive nor resistant. If something funny happens, laugh.

VARIATIONS

Do the opposite: fifteen minutes to plan something that will make us cry. Sometimes that's funnier. Both exercises can be assigned as overnight projects to give everyone a chance to plan more elaborate ideas with props, costumes, and choreography.

Trio Moments of Glory

This is a three-person version of moments of glory (see Chapter 2).

ACTION

Three people who are the best in the world at something enter, present their skill, and exit.

TECHNIQUE

Divide into trios, and take a day or two to prepare. Bring in the appropriate props and costumes for your presentation. Choreograph the entrance, presentation, and exit in a manner appropriate to your field of expertise. If it is an intellectual skill, do you enter and sit at a table? Or is it more Busby Berkely? Does one person speak more than the other two? Do you divide the presentation in thirds, or do you work in unison? Do you need music? Decide if you would like to take questions from the audience during your presentation. Make a piece that is two to five minutes long, silent or verbal. Allow the hierarchy of the group to develop out of your natural instincts to move, talk, lead, or follow. This is a nice exercise for working off of one another's strengths and weaknesses.

PITFALLS

Rehearse it. This doesn't work well if you have a funny idea and no presentation. Don't leave it all up to improv. Some very dry topics have worked beautifully because there was good commitment, good inter-action within the trio, and a good beginning, middle, and end. Bring in props. Memorable skills I have seen in class were the world's greatest hopscotchers, the world's best movers (furniture), the best spellers, and the world's greatest sympathy card writers, complete with cards.

VARIATIONS

Once every trio has performed, do another generation of development. Ask after each project: What worked? What went on too long? What could be developed further? Should there be more music, less music, or different music? Keep the best moments, add to the payoffs and the execution, and present it during the next class.

Action Etudes

ACTION

Three people create a short scene that accomplishes one clear action: They steal something, embarrass someone, surprise someone, betray someone, trick someone, or act out any provoking verb. They take fif-teen minutes to plan and choreograph it. They present it to class.

TECHNIQUE

Choose a playable action that does not need a lot of dialogue, so that the focus is on the timing and execution of the task. Use clear phrases, pauses, Ping-Pong, or whatever is needed to create suspense and ex-citement, and execute the action. This is a good way to explore verbs and find out what the difference is between an action that is mean, an action that is cruel, and an action that is funny.

PITFALLS

Focus on staging the moment of the action itself. Cut any exposition down to the minimum who/what/where needed. Etudes often fail be-cause the dialogue rambles, the action is weak, or it takes too long to get to the action.

After presenting the etudes once, get feedback on what would heighten the action, what would make it more cruel, what would make it more surprising, etc. Try it again. It usually works best to have two steal from one, or two being cruel to one, but you can flip it and have a single person steal from two.

Music Ideas

ACTION

Actors break into trios. They play sixteen bars of a simple, familiar, rhythmic piece of music on a CD, tape, or instrument. They repeat it a few times. I like to use '50s lounge music, like Esquival or Martin Denny. Each group needs to know the melody by heart. They choreograph an entrance and begin an activity that uses specific accents in the music. They play the music a few times for the groups to rehearse to. Each group presents their piece.

TECHNIQUE

Any half-baked idea is a good place to start. Use complex ideas or simple patterns of the expected, but make sure you hum the music out loud while rehearsing so that your actions fit the beat. Decide if you are using the music as background or doing physical actions that link directly to the accents in the music. Sid Caesar and Ernie Kovacs were masters at this. You don't need a complicated plot, you just need precision.

PITFALLS

If there is more than one idea, don't argue over what is best; try both. It's hard to rehearse several groups at the same time with only one tape recorder or CD. Give people time to memorize the music. Let each group rehearse with it while fine-tuning before looking at each group individually.

Assign the same activity to all of the trios. See what different solutions people come up with, using the same music. Try baking a cake, changing a flat tire, or performing an operation. Giving everyone the same task lets people see how many options there are in every action.

- Go beyond the sixteen-bar limit. Do a longer piece of music or a full song.

Food Ideas

Scenes with food have been a tradition in physical comedy since the beginning of time. Who knows what kind of horsing around at the campfire kept the tribe entertained. Food can be used in almost any of the exercises mentioned in this book. You can build a whole piece with food as the central theme. Putting food ideas on stage can be messy, but it's worth it if you don't mind cleaning up. The results can be hilarious.

ACTION

The class divides into groups of three. Each trio creates a piece that uses food. Each group has a day to go out, get the food item(s), and rehearse in private, making sure they plan for all possible problems of spillage, breakage, staining, and waste. They come back the next day and present all the pieces.

TECHNIQUE

I'm a great believer in just going for it, so there are no special steps to follow here. This exercise works well in groups of three or four actors, although more can be used. I require that each group must leave the space and the audience as clean as when they started and be responsible for bringing in the appropriate containers, coverings, floor protectors, and towels. If you're going to throw things, don't injure anyone. Soda is sticky; colored water isn't. Milk leaves a smell for days if it spills. Find a way to keep the mess contained.

PITFALLS

Make sure every action is rehearsed, even if it costs a little more to practice with the real items. Eggs, water, and other food items may not behave the way you imagine them to. Some items are cheaper to replace than others.

VARIATIONS

Give everyone the same three food items and a day to rehearse. See what each group does with a banana, a strawberry, and a loaf of bread, for instance. Music is optional.

That's it. Enjoy the results. Avoid humiliating someone in the audience without rewarding him or her. People have made whole careers out of smashing watermelons or eating twinkies, but the crowd will turn on you if you abuse their trust.

....5.Group Exercises

Any time there are more than three people on stage, you have a group. In groups, everyone needs to do less in order to do more. All of the following exercises are for fine-tuning group reflexes. It's best to work in groups of five or seven, to avoid falling into pairs. This chapter covers ensemble work, writing, and group improvisations.

The Group Ripple

ACTION

Everyone walks briskly around the room. A is "it." At random, A does an action and pauses. The instant anyone is aware of the action, he or she pauses and mirrors it.

TECHNIQUE

This is a warm-up that can be done with very large groups. After a few rounds, A should be able to stop, say "Wow!", and have everyone in the room do it a microsecond later in unison. As everyone mingles, give up trying to watch the leader. Trust that the ripple effect will get to you. You may see someone who saw someone else who was watching the person who saw the leader. As leader, change dynamics. Try softer, quieter actions, like pausing to discover a dead animal. Don't move again until the last person in the room has caught on and joined the pause. Change leaders after five or six rounds.

PITFALLS

Anticipating stops by watching the leader is boring; just mingle. Let your weight settle when you pause, so that your body is relaxed, open, and alert, not wound up with tension.

Build up to realistic situations such as a busy street corner with people coming and going. Have the leader notice a person standing on a window ledge ready to jump and the crowd join in seeing it. Play the scene.

The A–B–C Journey

ACTION

Three different places, or "stations," in the room are each assigned an action that the group does when they get there. For instance, at station A everyone leans against the wall in a row, at station B everyone stands center stage in a circle holding hands, at area C everyone lies on the floor with fingers in a straight line on the proscenium. In groups of five, actors start at one of these positions and move from one station to the next in any order, with no designated leader.

TECHNIQUE

This exercise is for listening, seeing, and moving as a group. Blend your impulses with everyone else's. Start slowly. Pick up on the smallest actions. Breathe together; amplify any little inclination to lean, to go to the floor, to jump, or to crawl. Make sure the group is with you and you are with the group. Some groups take two minutes to go from station to station, others rush from A to B to C several times. It doesn't matter how often you change stations, as long as no one appears to be pushing. Sound is allowed. Eventually it's quite meditative, like a large game of follow the leader with no leader and one set of evolving instincts.

PITFALLS

If everyone is too cautious, no one moves. If one person pushes all the time, it's not fair. Give it time. First, breathe. Each time the group gets to a station, the quality of the action can change. If the action is to jump, the group must jump at least once, but it can keep jumping as long as it wants until a new tangent occurs. The point is not to tag as many bases as possible. It's to realize every second that the journey is as interesting as the destination.

VARIATIONS

Three is an arbitrary number of stations. You could do a journey that has only one point, starting and ending at the same station.

Musical Associations

ACTION

All actors are on stage. An impressionistic or dramatic piece of music plays and actors visualize events. An actor calls an image out loud and everyone improvises that event. The actors let the image live for a minute. They use a whistle or bell to stop the action. The music keeps playing and someone calls out a different image. The actors play that scene. They continue jumping from scene to scene, mood to mood, and image to image. Each actor is allowed to find his or her own way to fit into the action.

TECHNIQUE

Not everyone can be central to every image. Play supporting roles, be on the sidelines, or provide counterpoint when that responsibility is thrust upon you. Opera, *Carmina Burana*, and certain instrumental pieces work well. Music with lyrics tends to limit the imagination, although Frank Sinatra works well. The person controlling the tape deck with the whistle needs to lower the volume of the music for people to be heard, then bring it back up to feed the energy between images. Some scenes can get quite noisy, and you have to jump in loudly to get people to drop back to neutral.

PITFALLS

Calling out too many scenes too quickly can cause trouble. Give the group time to explore the finer points of each image before moving on. Make sure all players let go of tension when they return to neutral.

Musical Brainstorms

ACTION

Everyone brings in a piece of music. They get into groups of three or five and listen to the pieces. Each group chooses one to work with. They discuss ideas for something that could be done using the music and develop a group piece. Each group presents their piece to the class. They get feedback, rehearse, and bring a revised piece in and present it the next day.

TECHNIQUE

None. This is an open forum for trying stuff out. Music may provide the inspiration, but it may have little to do with the final piece.

PITFALLS

Arguing over which piece of music to use is boring. Majority wins. Arguing over ideas is boring. Put more time into developing the idea than in discussing endless scenarios. Work through each step on your feet and try to combine brainstorms. If you have time to make two pieces, go for it.

VARIATIONS

Give everyone the same piece of music and a day to make a piece. See what everyone brings in. The music can be background, integral, or appear in the middle of the piece. It's up to each group.

Physical Comedy Writing

ACTION

Everyone writes out on a piece of paper a comic physical event. It can be a short idea or a very elaborate one. Writers should be specific about the number of people in it, who does what to whom, and what, if anything, is said. The number of performers can range from one to seven. Everyone puts the scenarios in a hat. Someone draws one out, picks the appropriate number of people to work on it, gives them twenty minutes to practice, and they present it.

TECHNIQUE

Read all the ideas out loud first. No names should be on the paper, so that no one knows whose idea it is. Choose an idea, get volunteers, and pick another idea until all people are working on something. Get three or four groups working at the same time. Give each group their written instructions to work with. No one can work on his or her own idea. Read the instructions out loud before presenting them. Watch the piece and discuss afterwards where it succeeded and where it failed. Get around to all of the ideas in the hat. Reveal whose idea it was, if you choose, at the very end.

This is different from that wonderful game show *Whose Line Is It Anyway*, where improvisers work from written instructions. In that show, the suggestions are bare-boned, and those brilliant improvisers take a dry idea and flesh it out fully. The skill here is to give complete instructions to the actors. Putting it in writing helps you step back from yourself and see what your ideas look like. Can someone else interpret your work? What do your ideas look like when you're not presenting them? Do other people bring a fresh approach? Did they do something you didn't expect?

PITFALLS

Be very specific. It is the only instruction people will get, and they can interpret freely any vague directions. This is another way of finding out what people think is funny. It's hard to write physical gags, which is why sitcoms rely so heavily on verbal repartee. Try not to give people impossible instructions to execute with only fifteen minutes of rehearsal, such as three actors fly in on airplane, crash land, and have their arm falls off, which they then eat. I've seen it happen, but it takes some prop preparation.

Grand Themes

ACTION

A group of seven or eight actors have an hour to go off and develop a piece with a beginning, middle, and end centering around a grand theme. They get back together and present the results. If there is more than one group, each group has the same theme.

TECHNIQUE

The only clue given is the open-ended theme, requiring an imaginative solution. Do with it what you will. The end result may need more than an hour of rehearsal, but the short time period often provokes interesting work. If the open-ended structure is too intimidating, appoint one person as narrator/oracle, and let everyone else physically present the story in story-theater fashion. Don't spend too much time writing complex dialogue. Think grandly. Use actors as props, the environment, the set, and characters. Interpret freely. The narrator can move things along and guide the action.

PITFALLS

This structure can lead to mythic and serious results. If it ends up being a beautiful piece instead of a funny one, consider that a good fringe benefit. *City Lights* is a very funny movie, but it is also very moving. I think Chaplin set out to move us more than he did to make us laugh, and the results speak for themselves.

VARIATIONS

Try any of the following themes, or make up your own.

- the creation of the world
- the last sip of water
- waiting on a road
- who's telling the truth
- the betrayal
- revenge of the animals
- the lonely one
- the first _____ (fill in the blank)
- the last _____ (fill in the blank)

Entrances and Exits

It's great fun to watch this exercise, and it needs an audience. If your class is huge, split in thirds. Otherwise, split in half so that you can serve as audience for each other.

ACTION

Using every possible exit or entrance in the playing area, the actors try never to have more than two people in the room at the same time (excluding the audience). As soon as a third arrives, someone has to leave. Everyone should do lots of entering and exiting. They run, walk, reverse direction, and crawl. They watch from the wings and use intuition to enter at the right moment. One group plays for about five minutes, then trades off and watches the other group work.

TECHNIQUE

Comedies are full of people coming and going. Use the space you are working in for what it is. Don't choose an imaginary setting such as a funeral home or a party. See what timing, momentum, expectations, and lots of people can do. If the room only has one door, set up a wing on either side of the stage so that you can go "off stage" to the left or right, and set up a center hiding place as well. This will give you three or four exits. Look for the right time to retreat, to stand still, or to use the floor. Find as many variables as possible. In the old Theater Funambules, made famous in *The Children of Paradise*, actors had to enter walking on their hands or on a tightrope in order to qualify as performers.

PITFALLS

Don't get chatty and involved in creating interesting scenes on stage. For the first time around just stay focused on entering and exiting as often as possible, fast/slow, forward/backward.

VARIATIONS

- Choose a setting, like a party or a funeral parlor. Get chatty and involved in creating an interesting scene, while still finding many reasons to exit and enter.

- Break the rule of two people at a time; allow everyone to be together now and then. Continue your part in the plot each time you appear. Try a dinner party where one person is avoiding another, a proposal is taking place, the food is late, a mysterious person keeps coming and going, and the host has the hiccups. Farce is built on these interlocking rhythms, and comedy has many of the same comings and goings.

Scales

These are exercises for dynamic range and for the ability to control the pitch and volume of an event with large numbers of people on stage. Group scales differ from duet escalations in that each player is more of a cog in the machine than a driving piston. Use states that are found when large numbers of people are together such as panic, celebration, or ritual. Practice the scale of fear, anger, drunkenness, anticipation, hunger, pride, laughter, or crying; any state that physically engages the breath, actions, and the voice will work well in a group. This as a form of calibrated calisthenics. It's a good idea to warm up first; get the breath going; play with actions that are suspended, relaxed, active, and malleable; use the floor; do some rolls; and get back up. Keep the group limber and expressive. Don't let these exercises go over the top with tension. In real life, any scale can lead to paralysis. On stage, you want to control the dynamic more carefully and stay just below that level of chaos.

ACTION

A group of seven actors is in the wings. One at a time they enter. Each person raises the stakes one notch on a given scale as he or she enters. The last person entering brings the group to a peak. When they leave, the state lowers a step at a time as the actors exit in the order they entered.

TECHNIQUE

Decide ahead of time what scale you are pursuing. Discuss the steps out loud. If you were doing the scale of laughter, what would be the first step? A twinkle in the eye? How quickly does it grow from a smile to a giggle to a chuckle to a laugh to full-scale hysteria? As you get to higher levels of energy, is it better for the group to be louder or quieter, banded together or farther apart? If there are five people, the steps are larger in order to peak by the fifth entrance. Each entering actor brings the next higher step on stage with him or her and infects the group. For the state to grow, each entrance must be timed so that the group's energy doesn't sag; however, silence on the way up can be used without a loss of energy. Use the other actors on stage to sustain the steps. Choose who enters first, second, third, and so on before starting. Rotate who comes in last with each exercise. The hardest job is jumping in at full throttle at the end. Entering actors should watch from the wings to see what will raise the stakes. People on stage need to be sensitive to the entering actor, especially on the highest steps, so that tensions are malleable and the last entrance gets noticed.

PITFALLS

It's very easy for one of the early entrances to bump the whole exercise too high, too quickly, leaving the last four people with a very small sliver of pie to divide up. Do logical steps (no curve balls), or you'll change the theme in the middle of the exercise. Try to hit a home run first. Do the *right* thing, rather than outwit the exercise. Also, the top of a scale often leaves people strangled with tension, unable to move. Stay just below that point, so that form and comprehension are still possible. Keep an eye out for richer choices, transcendent states that are quiet and powerful, or hilarious actions that still breathe. Each actor is responsible for a step, but not all steps are even. As you go up a scale, the steps accelerate. Don't wait too long to jump into the fray, or you'll leave your group out there dying. Some groups have a hard time getting going and may need to be remixed or given a new topic. Every group needs a prod to break through inhibitions; be brave if you want to play in the stratosphere.

VARIATIONS

1. Do the same exercise with everyone starting on stage sitting on a bench together. Have the scale passed across the line, bumped up by the end person, and passed back down the line using eye contact, gesture, and language. The people in the middle need to sustain the state without raising or lowering it.

The end people turn out to the audience, raise the state, and pass it on. This pattern usually breaks down toward the top, and anyone who feels there is a greater height to be reached can escalate the situation.

2. Allow the scale to metamorphose after the peak. Rather than exit or go back down the scale, let the group find a new common direction; head that way on a new theme. Don't preplan what it will be; just pay attention to the group. The scale of anticipation might turn into the scale of disappointment, the scale of fear, or the scale of coughing. After two or three rounds, trade groups. It's tremendously draining, and people need to rest after such a roller coaster.

3. A great way to turn scales into practical scenarios is to go back to the version with entrances and make the last person who enters the *reason* for the escalating state. For example, if there are five people doing the scale of fear, the fifth person entering is the object of their fear. If eight people are doing the scale of anticipation, the seventh is the last step before the object of anticipation (the queen, the president, the hero, or the angel) enters. At that point let a new scale carry you. Beg the queen for forgiveness; when she leaves, another scale can be played out such as the scale of loss, the scale of revolt, or the scale of resignation. Do one scale up, another down to find an ending.

4. Repeat variation 3, only play out the full scenario with many scales up and down, but always one theme at a time. Play the concert, start the game, begin the trial, get married, be sacrificed, or start class—see how many opportunities appear. Interruptions, escalations, and Ping-Pong will abound. Allow duets and trios to play out, use the other characters on stage as sounding boards, allies, or people who make entrances and exits that build tension. Find an ending. At this point, you're awfully close to doing a full-scale play without the script. Go to variation 5.

5. Find a scripted scene that uses several characters to build to a climax. Cast it, learn the dialogue, and decide what scale the

author asks for. Is it a scale of dread or eagerness? See if you can play it as written, creating the build, while staying alert to any subplots within the situation. Play the dialogue with great awareness of the total effect you have on each other chemically.

6. An important structure to practice is two directions at once. Choose one person who escalates in a different direction from the group, for instance, a groom giving a speech at his wedding. Start simply, but have all the guests gradually build a crescendo of catcalls while the host tries to be sincere. He does a scale of frustration and disappointment, while they do a scale of drunken camaraderie. One scale drives the other in perfect counterpoint, and the joy of six equals the misery of one. Never let the group get so out of control that all dramatic structure breaks down. It becomes less interesting. Try playing a serious lecturer with a class that gradually notices his or her pants are on backwards (preset them that way so the reactions are genuine). Start simple, use the ripple effect, feel whether it's a scale of laughter versus embarrassment or anger versus guilt. Try a priest with the hiccups and a congregation trying to maintain solemnity.

Staging Bedlam

In many plays, farces, and comedies, interweaving themes come to a head in a climactic scene, often at the end of Act II or III. For instance, the antagonist starts a conflict, gets interrupted by a duel, wakes up the drunk in the corner who collides with the in-laws arriving, all while someone announces they have a bomb. This is bedlam.

ACTION

The climactic scene of any comedy or farce with a large cast.

TECHNIQUE

A simple technique for dealing with these colliding themes is to take each actor and work his or her role individually, reacting to all of the comings and goings alone on stage, with the stage manager calling the lines. Go all the way to the end, playing with flight paths and reactions, even though no one else is entering or exiting. Then add one person at a time, in the order in which they appear in the play, and repeat the scene. Do the whole scene with two people, then three, and so on. Have the other actors watch. As you add each new player, he or she can build on the paths of the other actors. Very complex patterns of coming and going, stepping over or running into someone can be worked out one move at a time.

Once everyone has had a chance to see what his or her role in the chaos is, rehearse the whole scene slowly, gradually picking up the tempo until the illusion of bedlam is complete. Make any changes needed to further interlock the actions or fine-tune moments. Once the whole class can safely play the scene, additional moments can be layered in for pizzazz. In a production of *The Coconuts* at the Actors Theater of Louisville, Jon Jory did a masterful job staging the classic Marx Brothers hotel scene with doors opening and closing with split-second timing. He said they spent forty hours on that sequence alone, and it was worth it. The illusion of a catastrophe on stage is the result of a smoothly functioning internal harmony, unseen by the audience, created by every actor being acutely aware of his or her part within the greater whole, orchestrated carefully through rehearsal.

Pitfalls

Lack of rehearsal time and too much tension in the actors' bodies can interfere with the successful timing and execution of bedlam. When it works, a good comedy resembles a brilliantly played basketball game, with smooth coordination between all the players creating the illusion of ease and spontaneity.

Variations

Rather than run each actor separately, break the scene into ten-second units and run each unit in phrases, saying go and stop, like the game red light, green light. This lets the actors see where they need to be and reinforces a sense of balance and control over the event. Use a drum or a bell to cue the stopping and starting of actions. Anyone caught in midair is allowed to land on stop.

- Run the scene at half tempo, and pick it up gradually. Repeat the trickiest phrases a few times in a row until they run smoothly.
- If you are in a show with a very large cast, divide the actors into teams according to function, and rehearse them separately, e.g., the middle-of-the-room team, the cops team, the frightened-patrons team. Then combine the groups.
- Run the whole scene focusing on one element: entrances and exits, prop manipulation, space between actors, softest point/loudest point, and so on. Insert one cue that everyone hits. In the exploding fireworks scene in *You Can't Take It with You*, I once placed a pause in the middle of all the explosions. I had everyone sigh as if it were over, then did a second round of bombs for the finale. It worked well.

Summary

Every show presents its own challenges, but here are some general principles for directors and actors working with comedic scripts.

Give yourself plenty of rehearsal time, and be off-book before you begin. You need your hands free and your minds open. I prefer six to seven weeks of rehearsal for a full-length script and five to six months for an original piece. Do your dramaturgical research to find a vigorous and appropriate interpretation of the world of the play. Personalize the problems the author has given you and then interpret them physically. If you're supposed to be in love, find a way to show it and mean it. But if you are the lovers in *Coconuts*, forget it, don't belabor it. You are a plot device and a foil for the Marx Brothers' zaniness. You need to understand that and adjust your instincts to fit the role accordingly. Comic plots are often extremely unrealistic.

You can be a great actor who's a lousy comic, but you can't be a great comic if you aren't a great actor. Compare Zero Mostel to Jim Varney (Ernest). Err more towards Zero than Jim. Make sure the business you develop is appropriate to the play. As Hamlet advises the players, "Suit the action to the word, the word to the action." Beware of false actions and reactions. Give yourself time in rehearsal to explore the main themes on your feet. Shakespeare is full of clues for the actions he wants you to find. Mark through the physical business every night, just as you would do a combat call in a show that is violent. Keep adjusting business until the show closes. Running the show with a live audience teaches you grace in execution and timing.

The largest, most chaotic scenes require the most detail and rehearsal. Putting inappropriate shtick on top of a climax will smother it. Comedy should arise out of your heartfelt efforts to value the world of the play and engage in its dilemmas, not a desire to invent comic clutter. Don't fall in love with any ideas. Whatever you do, work safely. No moment on stage is worth a career-ending injury. Avoid props made of glass, sharp objects, objects that are too heavy to maneuver, out of control or off-balance actions, and the placement of any body part between a moving and a nonmoving object. Nuff said. Have fun, even if it kills you in rehearsal to get to that point. They don't call them "plays" for nothing!

···6· Advice to the Players

In 1995 I spoke with Jacques Lecoq, a leading authority on movement training, physical theater, and founder of the Ecoles Jacques Lecoq in Paris, France. I was attending a summer workshop on the pedagogy of the school and explained to Monsieur Lecoq that I was working on a book about theater training. I asked him what advice he would give to young people interested in studying physical comedy. He replied:

> First and foremost I would tell them never to lose their curiosity. Curiosity about the structures of life and life's phenomena. Then I would tell them to nurture the joy of play and the pleasure of performance. In order to re-create life on stage we must feed off everyday life and nature. These are the two great sources of acting. Then they should discover how to mime all this with their body, always striving to be as true as possible to life as we know it.
>
> The important thing is not how many ideas they may have but their ability to ground them, to plant them in something living which speaks to us and with which we can identify. Yes, be curious about life.
>
> In the expression of all this, beware of formalism and sectarianism. Go for what is most interesting, the most living expression of what they want to say. Beware of aesthetic formulations. Go for the inner sources of style so that it grows from within and is not merely stuck onto the surface of the performance.
>
> We all tend to look for security. But nothing is fixed, engraved forever in tablets of stone. Everything must be put in question.
>
> Errors are necessary in any teaching method. Accept them, learn from them.

Sound advice. Since that discussion I learned that Lecoq has published a book about his work, in French, called *Le Corps Poétique*. It is slated for translation into English in 1999 by Methuen Drama of London. For a thorough understanding of his work, I highly recommend you find a copy.

I also conducted interviews with three teachers and performers of physical comedy, Avner Eisenberg, Geoff Hoyle, and Ronlin Foreman, to give you some idea of their training paths and their approaches to comedy. The first interview is with Geoff Hoyle, who toured with the Pickle Family Circus and has appeared in numerous Broadway and off-Broadway productions, including *The Lion King*. Next is Avner Eisenberg, a.k.a. Avner the Eccentric, familiar to many as the Jewel in Michael Douglas' film the *Jewel of the Nile*, and a solo clown who tours internationally. The final interview is with Ronlin Foreman, a solo clown and teacher of clown and fool at the Dell'Arte school in California.

Geoff Hoyle

DR   How did you get started in physical comedy?

GH   It was part of growing up for me. We were always doing skits and bits, kidding around at parties, weddings, funerals, with my cousins, aunts, and uncles—one of the things my dad would do was imitate comedians and then laugh himself.

DR   Things he'd seen in shows?

GH   Yes, in shows, pantomimes . . .

DR   You're English. Were pantomimes still going on then?

GH   Pantos? They still are now. That whole tradition came out of commedia, Grimaldi, Punch and Judy, the Music Hall. It was part of my family life, seeing comic performers in pantos, stage shows, and on the television. The equivalent here in America might be people like Jackie Gleason, Art Carney, Dick Van Dyke, Phil Silvers. Later, I watched the great silent movie comedians. When I was in Paris studying with Decroux there was a Keaton retrospective at the cinemathèque . . .

DR   When was this?

GH   This was 1968, after a degree at Birmingham University in England in drama and English literature. I was very enamored of iconoclastic theater and performers and of playwrights like Brecht, since he was in love with music hall and cabaret. I'd always loved those forms and studied them as much as I could. As an actor, I had a certain physical adeptness. I had done things like Beckett's *Act Without Words* and done very well at theaters and festivals in England and France. I asked one of my mentors, Clive Barker, what I should do. He suggested I go to France and get some training "from the horse's mouth." And I said, "Well, is it going to be Lecoq or Decroux?" and the choice became very simple. First of all, Clive said the master was Decroux, and second of all, Lecoq's school was three times the price, so I went to Decroux's on a French government grant and studied for two years.

When I came back I started working in a street theater company, the Dogg's Troupe, part of a group called Inter-Action. Again, this work was based on popular forms. I went back to the great silent-film comedians; they're really a gift because they are *there*. They are on record, you can rent their films in video stores and you can buy them.

DR   Many of those comedians trained at the turn of the century; it seems likely that their technique originated in the nineteenth century, and you are watching material that goes back two hundred years or more.

GH   I believe that's more like two thousand. . .

DR   I didn't know you worked with Decroux. So many people who worked with him do very cerebral work. You seem much more "salt of the earth."

GH   Good, that's always been my intention! Decroux's aesthetic is bifurcated—he talked constantly about "art," "the abstract," "beauty." But at the same time he wanted to tell touching and hilarious stories about prostitutes he had known or great popular singers. Many people take only the serious side and run with it; there are those who imitate Decroux and are more like Decroux than Decroux. My tendency is to take the technique and apply it retroactively to the popular forms.

Performers in European popular culture, the mimes of the Middle Ages and early 1800s like Debureau, and later European clowns like Pipo, Rhum, Marceline, Grock, probably had intuitive techniques that were similar to Decroux's. It was Decroux who stepped back and codified them. I was always conscious that I was going to take the technique to fuel my abilities to do the popular stuff. I wasn't going to "do Decroux." I respected him, but I knew that popular comedy was where I wanted to go because I was so influenced by Keaton, Chaplin, and Langdon, and by the performers I had seen on television— physical, funny, surreal. *The Goon Show* was around then, people like Peter Sellers, Michael Bentine, and Tommy Cooper, a hysterically, terrifyingly, sad comedian, and Max Wall, one of the last of the great music-hall variety comics who had made their living on stage, just touring and doing pantos. Some of them are still doing it. Most of them are on their way out.

DR   I think they used to pop up on Ed Sullivan. Is there anyone comparable in this country?

GH   Well, you've got people from vaudeville, burlesque, radio, television. America has Jack Benny, Harpo Marx, Art Carney, Danny Kaye, Lucille Ball!

DR   Who is that brilliant old-timer who gets his hands stuck in his clothes? There is just a little bit of footage of him in that movie . . .

GH   George Carl in *Funny Bones*? That's a wonderful movie— flawed, strange, very mad. I worked with George Carl once at a new vaudeville festival put on at San Francisco State University. He was amused at the "festival" concept, didn't know what all the fuss was about. On the way from the airport he kept asking if they'd got the right guy. I think it's important for institutions like colleges to gather these people together and focus on their work before they can no longer do it. Hire physical comedians for workshops, commission artists, organize the study of popular arts and performance.

DR   Any advice to the players?

GH   Having seen all these guys on television and having worked and appropriated their bits (I call it borrowing), I say to people do anything they do, but do it your way. Don't just imitate. You have to take the work and transform it, using it as a basis. All artists do that. You learn from the masters and transform the material so it becomes something new.

Street performing is great training. That's getting harder and harder because so many of the public spaces you want to work in are now private. Or you have to audition, which is completely antithetical to what street work is about: showing up and creating an exciting, anarchic event.

I have had the most fun recently working in universities with students that have a genuine interest in the material. The aim of actor training can't be just Oscars and Emmys and Tonys.

DR   Do you see any hope on the national level?

GH   Many experimenters of the '60s and '70s have moved into more established areas, like the regional nonprofit theater. *The Convict's Return*, my last solo show, went to several regional theaters. They are often able to commission new work, or co-produce, or offer a touring network. It's economically viable, especially if you can negotiate a percentage of the gross as a writer.

International festivals are another place to go, especially for physical performers who don't rely on words. There are festivals in Canada, where they still support the popular arts, Eastern Europe, Australia, Asia, and I think there are untapped venues in South America. You can get more information from the Dell'Arte school. They've gone to Caracas, Venezuela, for a number of years. They say it is wild. It sounds like the '60s. There is so much of a love for theater and live performance down there.

As for training, there are circus arts schools still operating in the former Soviet Union with some amazing trainers. In this country, Pickle Family Circus has a circus school in San Francisco. There's the circus school in France: Centre Nationale des

Arts du Cirque in Chalons. The Lecoq school in Paris. Dimitri's school in Switzerland. There is the National Circus School of Canada in Montreal, where Cirque du Soleil gets a lot of their best people—it's almost their farm system. Any kind of physical work you can do helps—dance, martial arts. Plus acting training, of course. I tell people, whenever I'm acting I'm not necessarily clowning, but whenever I'm clowning, I'm always acting.

DR   You also have strong vocal technique, as was obvious in *The Lion King.*

GH   You have to have a trained voice, absolutely. And I think you have to train your *ear* as well as your voice. Mimicry is a useful technique. Imitating people's voices, animals, machines, sounds in nature. Look at Jonathan Winters! It's useful to learn to play an instrument, too. I learned violin when I was young, and I've kept it up. I'm not a brilliant violinist, but I can knock out a few tunes. You don't have to become a virtuoso, and it's useful to have music theory. Even a deceptively simple instrument like a recorder or a cymbal and a drum is great. When we had the street troupe we were playing on all sorts of stuff. Coffee cans, banjo, accordion, and brass instruments.

DR   That's a good point. Music is such a part of physical comedy.

GH   Music and musicality. It's all about rhythm. Italian playwright Dario Fo once said to me, "Theatre *is* rhythm."

The other thing I would say to people is be aware of the tradition, find out about it through movies, books. It's important to acknowledge the traditions. It deepens the work.

DR   It's hard to find resource materials. Any recommendations for where to look?

GH   It's there, you can find it. It's academic study, it's photo research. You need to go to archives like Lincoln Center's Library of the Performing Arts. Look up photographs, engravings, letters, first-hand descriptions of work. Find John Towsen's book *Clowns*, Allardyce Nicoll's *Masks, Mimes, and Miracles*, Maurice Disher's *Clowns & Pantomimes*, and Duchartre's *The Italian Comedy*, or consult Raymond Toole-Stott's *Circus & Allied*

Arts: A World Bibliography. Hovey Burgess, circus expert and historian extraordinaire, is here in New York. Clown expert and teacher Larry Pisoni is in the Seattle area.

DR   I've tried to avoid rules in this book that anyone might construe as "the right way" to be funny, since it's such an individual process.

GH   Well, you can deduce certain rules empirically from what you observe and by doing it. But beware, comedy is about *breaking* rules. If you work in comedy you have a comic vision or you don't. Everybody has a sense of humor at some point, but people who successfully work in comedy have a comic take on life. Paradoxically, it's a way of easing the pain, of surviving. I wouldn't be the first to say that behind all great comedy lies tragedy. Maybe because life isn't comic, it's tragic. Comedy is a reaction to the tragedy. That's why I love Beckett's work and why I jumped at the chance to do Clov in *Endgame*. It's such a desperate, poignant piece, and very funny.

Avner Eisenberg

DR   How did you get interested in the tradition of physical comedy, and how did you get your training?

AE   My interest in physical comedy began with my interest in theater. I started college as a chemistry major. In my first year, I got disenchanted with chemistry, caught mononucleosis, and quit school. When I came back, it was as a humanities major. One day, I ducked out of a thunderstorm into the theater building and got a small part in a commedia production of the *Mandragola* by Machiavelli. This first exposure to commedia was key to my interest in physical comedy.

I saw Marcel Marceau perform in New York, and soon after started writing and performing silent sketches in whiteface. When I started to grow a beard, I became a tramp clown and added several more skills to the mime work: juggling, acrobatics, magic, and puppetry. After college, I went to Paris to study with Lecoq. At first, it was very difficult. I had gone to Lecoq's thinking it was a mime school and that I could learn to be like Marceau. I had wanted to study with Marceau but couldn't find an address for his school. Luckily, Lecoq was listed in the Paris phone book, so I went there instead. After about two months at the school, I had an awakening to Lecoq's system and to the depth of his work. Lecoq often said that we would really begin to learn about theater after we had finished the school and that he was more interested in where we would be in five years than in how we did as students. So, I finished the two years at the school and my education began in earnest.

I tried to perform as often as possible at every imaginable venue: birthday parties, opening for music acts, in the street, and in every fair, festival, and benefit that would have me. After a year or two, I settled into the Renaissance Fair circuit, where I was known as the guy with the ten-minute rope-walking act who would do anything to avoid doing it. I had a series of seemingly improvised digressions that led up to a modest display of rope walking. While working at the fairs, I continued to perform at colleges and clubs and gradually developed the show that later went to New York.

DR   What advice do you have for people studying physical comedy?

AE   Always remember, if you can't succeed every time, learn to fail magnificently. So much of physical comedy is a celebration of small failures, so don't be afraid of failure; rather, embrace it. W. C. Fields said something to the effect that comedy is tragedy happening to someone else. To do physical comedy, in a sense, one becomes that someone else. Ashley Montague responded to the question of how he managed to be so interesting by saying that it was easy: One merely had to be interested. The clown and physical comedian must always remain interested and fascinated, never losing their curiosity and sense of play.

I think that physical comedy is a folk art in the sense that it really must be learned from a teacher, or a mentor. It absolutely cannot be learned from a book. My advice is to find a teacher whose style you admire.

DR   Any suggestions for where to study?

AE   There are three places: the Celebration Barn, in South Paris, Maine. The Barn offers a series of one- and two-week workshops from June to September. The offerings vary from year to year, but for the past four years have included several mime and storytelling workshops with Tony Montanaro, Stage Combat, Roy Hart Voice Technique, and clowning, taught by Julie Goell and myself. The Dell'Arte school, in Blue Lake, California, offers a yearlong program in physical theater. And of course, there is the Lecoq school in Paris, France.

DR   What about your own teaching? How did you get started, and what do you teach?

AE   For many years I taught workshops based on what I learned from Lecoq, Carlo Mazzone Clementi (founder of the Dell'Arte school), and other teachers of mine. However, I resisted teaching clown. Finally, at the urging of Joan Schirle at Dell'Arte, I agreed to develop a course. For the first time, I was able to define themes and develop exercises that derived both from my own performances and from my work as a writer-director. I taught clown for several years at Dell'Arte, and for the past four or five years I have been teaching a yearly two-week workshop at the Celebration Barn.

At first it was a struggle, but over time a pedagogy emerged. My ideas about clown are largely based on Lecoq's clown, but also draw on concepts like *complicity* from Phillipe Gaulier, and *status* from Keith Johnstone. Some of the ideas I try to teach are that the clown *is* the material, your clown needs complicity with the audience to even exist, and clowning happens while waiting for something else to happen. Most of the exercises are derived from themes abstracted both from my own performances and work I've done with others as a cowriter-director.

The beginning of every class or workshop is a series of exercises dealing with personal comfort. It has been my experience that most people are somewhat uncomfortable on stage, even people who perform a lot. They are often unaware of their own discomfort. The first series of exercises are designed to allow one to become sensitized to one's own subtle levels of discomfort and lead them into a state of comfort on stage.

DR I remember taking a clowning workshop with you, and you spent a great deal of time working on breath and action. It was fascinating.

AE Breathing is not only the basis of life, it is also important in comedy. Exhalation is a physical expression of comfort and completion. Holding one's breath is an expression of effort or defense. Often defensiveness of the actor is interpreted as defensiveness of the character. It is important to be sensitive to one's breath, for what feels like an insignificant nuance reveals the truth of our feelings to the audience. In my own work, both performing and directing, I often look closely at the breathing in the search for an adjustment that will make something be funny. From the breathing comes comfort, and comfort is the beginning of the clown work.

I use many exercises from Aikido to teach breathing and economical movement. Aikido teaches you to move in ways that maintain your balance, comfort, and awareness.

DR What about failure? Should clowns fail in a certain way, get into frustrating situations, have things break or go wrong?

AE Failure certainly has an important place in clowning. But for failure to work as a tactic it must be fresh and never forced. The trick is to make accidents seem as if they've never happened before.

DR And be genuinely surprised.

AE Yes, and the clown must be very accepting. The clown must be oriented to the future so that his or her reaction is never mired in psychological memory. In the face of adversity, the clown's attitude is one of optimism, hope, and naiveté. These things can't be learned from books.

DR No they can't. I hope if anything this book will trigger people to find teachers. We went mad after each class with Lecoq trying to scribble things down, because we knew you couldn't find this work in a book, and he didn't allow notebooks in class.

AE   He wanted you to experience it.

DR   Thanks Avner, it was good talking with you.

Ronlin Foreman

DR   How did you get started in physical theater?

RF   When I was in kindergarten, I saw a production of *Beauty and the Beast* on TV. I think it might have been that series hosted by Shirly Temple Black. The thing that was most fertile for me was that Beauty was in this huge dining hall waiting for the Beast to come in, and as the Beast approached, you heard footsteps thundering through the palace. You saw nothing, but you *surmised* what the approach of the Beast must mean just by what you heard.

For me, the work of theater, of physical theater, is the production of a fertile suggestion. That is power. It is what has provoked me about scenic design as well, the whole nature of presenting an image, an event. It is why I didn't just go into acting and conventional theater. I'm really interested in presenting to an audience that *mystery* (i.e., the sound of the footsteps approaching). There must be a significant enigma, a poignant enigma, but an enigma that is not cloudy or ill-shaped. And yet, an enigma that is too narrative or too defined also kills. Give the audience an irony to scuffle with, to wrestle with, like Jacob and the angel. That's what interested me initially—that sense of mystery in performance.

I went back to kindergarten the next day, set up a row of chairs, and I stomped along the chairs over and over for everybody. There was no ascent or descent with the chairs; they were in a straight line. But there was a sense of the spaces between the sounds. And that's important: the space between the action, the moments of stillness. It's a hallmark of the work that I do and one that I look for in my directing and teaching as well.

When I think back on it, it was a very compulsive, sort of demented thing I did (stomping on chairs), but the teacher thought it was pretty impressive and wrote on the card at the end of the year, "Ronnie will probably go into theater."

DR   Did you start doing theater in college?

RF   Yes. At first I majored in scenic design, but after taking some classes in oral interpretation, acting, and modern dance, I changed to a performance emphasis. I also took some teaching courses and actually began teaching mime while I was still in school. The teaching helped me as a way of learning—a way of seeing, finding things. This has been very helpful to me as a director and as a performer.

DR   When did your solo career start?

RF   After my sophomore year in college I toured with a national company, the Everyman Players. And although I did traditional ensemble work with them, they also gave me the opportunity to do featured mimetic solo pieces. I continued for about ten years to do ensemble and solo work with various companies such as the Sheffield Ensemble Theatre and the Nashville Children's Theatre. It was while serving as the director of creative dramatics with NCT that I gave my first full evening's solo performance. I had been exposed to and participated in a wide range of theatrical styles, but in 1980, I threw all of my eggs in one basket and began to focus on a solo career in physical theater. I really liked physical theater because of its suggestive nature, not so much the explicit pantomime work that I ended up dropping by the wayside. I was enamored with Decroux's work, but didn't see myself committing to years of studying it as a discipline.

In New York I met a teacher who had been a student of Lecoq's. I remember one time sitting around the dark edges backstage listening to what she was doing with her students—the work with the clown, the nature of the child, and the nature of play. After that I went to a big festival in LaCrosse, Wisconsin, where Lecoq was teaching a master class and I ended up going to Paris to study with him.

I liked improvisation, the spontaneity, how an image developed, how a perfect arrangement of time, space, and action can be achieved, not out of stylization or rudiment, but through an intense devotion to character.

DR   Is that one of the things that has kept you teaching?

RF   Yup. And the fact that I've been asked to!

It also informs my directing. The teaching work has a polarity, to look deeper into the students for a point of origin, their gifts. And on the other end, to hold as strongly as possible to a kind of play that I know intuitively works, and that can be combined with their gifts. The last four or five years have been a terrific time of really pushing the bounds of that.

DR   In Nashville?

RF   No, at Dell'Arte. All the workshops there culminate in student performances. I try to take them deeper into the work of thematics, deeper into the work of the metaphor, deeper into the work of the fool. That's a nice thing about the school. The work there isn't just theoretical. Everyone is expected to produce, and at the end of each section of study there is a cumulative showing of their work. After they've finished the full year of study, they do a two-week tour in the community. The students must do the publicity, the contacting, the scheduling. It's a complete division of labor and a good transition to starting a career.

DR   What advice do you have for people interested in studying physical comedy?

RF   Some people have a hard time understanding this, but I feel like the individual must be reduced to a point of "not having," of "not knowing." When they've reached this point they are vulnerable. But it's not a sentimental vulnerability. It's a poverty that offers—necessitates—new inventions. They are in a position where what they produce is, and really will be, a surprise to them. Creating moments that are genuinely new, not something they've relied on in the past. It doesn't always happen for everyone; that's the hardest lesson. It's not always easy for the student because I haven't always been able to say exactly what it is that I am looking for.

DR   I think students can sense that you look deeply into who they are and what they can accomplish without just passing on a sequence of tricks.

RF   Bruce Mars, a teacher at Dell'Arte, says that after years of hearing it, he has now learned my orientation speech to the students. "I don't know anything, I'm not going to teach you any tricks. I'm a provocateur. My availability to you is my eye."

DR   I certainly saw people do things in the Through the Roof exercise in your workshop that I haven't seen anywhere else.

RF   That's a Lecoq minimum-to-maximum exercise, and it's typical of the work I ask people to do now in my clown classes. It's why teaching in the realm of the clown is so interesting. Not for everyone to *be* a clown. It is a form that requires the dimension to be *greater* than people can imagine. It takes a dimension and stretches it as far as the individual's capacity to deal with it. And it deals with the absurd and surrealism, so the context is relative in the play of it. Few people have the energy at first to press into the realm I ask for.

DR   Are you interested anymore in pursuing that realm as a performer, or only through teaching?

RF   I don't know if I'll ever return to performing. It requires a lot of sacrifices of family, finances, and after twenty years, it was enough. Right now, my great passion is raising my three children. And the work of teaching and directing is very rewarding. It allows me to step out of the center and to visualize and propose an entire universe that is a whole integration of all of the elements: time, space, physical forms, sound, and action. All of that remains a great passion for me.

Random Notes

Lou Jacobs', a great clown and teacher at Ringling Brothers Clown College, standard admonishment to students whose work was sloppy was, "That's spaghetti!"

Stan Laurel: "What is comedy? I don't know. Does anybody? Can you define it? All I know is that I learned to get laughs, and that's all I know about it. You have to learn what people will laugh at, and proceed accordingly."

One of the best training films for comedy is a BBC series called *The Unknown Chaplin*. In it, you see Chaplin being *unfunny*, changing setups, getting frustrated, searching for actions that best suit the theme he is exploring or the environment he is playing in.

Chris Wink, founding member of Blue Man Group: "The process here flows out of our relationships. It was really very much like sitting around saying, 'Wouldn't it be cool if we did . . .' But then we actually had a meeting and made shit happen. Instead of just sitting there and smoking cigarettes, we kept blending the bohemian hanging out with actually having a to-do list and making phone calls and hammering nails."

George Carl's script for an eight-minute, silent routine performed in 1983 for the Queen of England:

> Enter (rushin ballet).
> Biz. with mic, biz. with wire
> Adjust dress, biz. with no pockets.
> Hat off, bow, hit mic.
> Jacket roll-over.
> Hat rolls.
> More biz. with wire, thumb in button hole, wrestle with braces, thumb in eye.
> Biz. with sleeves (long/short)
> Fetch table, trap thumb.
> Adjust mic. (again), play mouth organ
> Biz. with foot (lost control).
> Biz with gum, stuck to mic, pocket, foot, tongue.

Play "Honeysuckle Rose." Band plays "Can-Can."
Mouth-organ falls apart.
Biz. with table (too heavy).
Off.

Two minutes to read, a lifetime to master.

Avner once mentioned four points in a workshop that I've always found useful for making good theater. They are: joy, skill, risk, and momentum.

Bounce the Clown, a street performer who was one of my earliest juggling teachers, once said, "It's easy to make people laugh. All you have to do is fall down and make funny faces." As a teacher, I like to work with more complex theories of performance, but through the years the fact is, Bounce's law is often true. Sometimes, just fall down and make funny faces.

The great playwright and director George Kaufman was rehearsing one of his plays when a young actor took a long pause midsentence. When Kaufman asked the actor why he put such a long pause in the middle of the sentence, the actor replied "Well Mr. Kaufman, in the script there was the first part of the sentence, then eight dots on the page, and then the second part." Kaufman replied, "Next time, try three dots."

Los Trios Ringbarkus, an Australian absurdist clown duet: "Sorry about the mess. . . . Sorry about the smell. . . ."

Appendix

Addresses, Resources, and Performers

If you would like hands-on training, here are the addresses of some of the major schools and performers currently conducting workshops.

Ecole Jacques Lecoq
57, Rue du Faubourg Saint-Denis
75010 Paris, France

The Dell'Arte School
PO Box 816
Blue Lake, CA 95525
707-668-5663

The Celebration Barn Theater
RFD 1 Box 236
South Paris, ME 04281
(Workshops with Avner Eisenberg, Julie Goell, myself, and others)

The Center for Movement Theater
Dodi DiSanto, director
PO Box 11655
Washington, DC 20008
301-495-8822

Antonio Fava
Teatro Dell Vicolo
C.P. 404
42100 Reggio-Emilia, Italy
Fax: 011-39-522-455589

Workshops may also be offered by:

Theatre De La Jeune Lune
105 First Street, N.
Minneapolis, MN 55401
612-333-6200

Ecole Phillipe Gaulier
PO Box 1815
London, England N51BG
Tel.: 01-71-249-6288

Theatre de Complicite
20-24 Eden Grove
London, England N7 8ED
Tel.: 01-71-700-0233

John Rudlin
Selavy
Grosbout
16240 La Foret de Tesse, France

Here is a partial list of companies known for doing physical work who may also offer workshops on occasion:

Theatre du Soliel
Robert LePage
Peter Brook
Theater de la Jeune Lune
Pilobolus
Big Apple Circus

You can contact me at:

Davis Robinson
Department of Theater and Dance
9100 College Station
Bowdoin College
Brunswick, ME 04011
207-772-9924
drobinso@bowdoin.edu
www.beaujest.com

Bibliography

Actor's Theater of Louisville. 1990. *Commedia Dell'Arte & the Comic Spirit*. Louisville: Actor's Theater of Louisville.

Atkins, Greg. 1994. *Improv! A Handbook for the Actor*. Portsmouth, NH: Heinemann.

Bergson, Henri. 1911. *Laughter*. New York: MacMillan.

Bermel, Albert. 1982. *Farce*. New York: Simon & Schuster.

Brook, Peter. 1984. *The Empty Space*. New York: Atheneum.

Burns, George. 1989. *All My Best Friends*. New York: G. P. Putnam's Sons.

Caesar, Sid. 1983. *Where Have I Been?* New York: Signet.

Cahn, William. 1957. *The Laugh Makers*. New York: Bramhall House.

Chaplin, Charles. 1964. *My Autobiography*. New York: Simon & Schuster.

Disher, Maurice. 1968. *Clowns and Pantomimes*. North Stratford, NH: Arno Press.

Duchartre, Pierre Louis. 1966. *The Italian Comedy*. New York: Dover.

Felheim, Marvin. 1972. *Comedy*. New York: Harcourt Brace.

Felner, Mira. 1985. *Apostles of Silence*. Cranbury, NJ: Farleigh Dickinson University Press.

Goldstein, Malcolm. 1979. *George Kaufman*. New York: Oxford University Press.

Grock. 1969. *Life's a Lark*. New York: Benjamin Blom.

Honri, Peter. 1973. *Working the Halls*. Farnborough, England: Saxon House.

Hopper, DeWolf. 1927. *Once a Clown, Always a Clown*. Boston: Little, Brown.

Johnstone, Keith. 1979. *Impro: Improvisation and the Theatre*. New York: Theater Arts Books.

Jones, Chuck. 1989. *Chuck Amuck*. New York: Farrar, Strauss & Giroux.

Kerr, Walter. 1975. *The Silent Clowns*. New York: Alfred A. Knopf.

Lahr, John. 1969. *Notes on a Cowardly Lion*. New York: Alfred A. Knopf.

Leabhardt, Thomas. 1989. *Modern and Post-Modern Mime*. London: Macmillan.

Lecoq, Jacques. 1987. *Le Theatre du Geste*. Paris: Bordas.

Maltin, Leonard. 1970. *Movie Comedy Teams*. New York: Signet.

Martinez, J. D. 1982. *Combat Mime*. Chicago: Nelson Hall.

Marx, Arthur. 1954. *Life with Groucho*. New York: Simon & Schuster.

Marx, Harpo, with Rowland Barber. 1985. *Harpo Speaks!* New York: Proscenium Publishers.

Mast, Gerald. 1973. *The Comic Mind*. Chicago: University of Chicago Press.

McNamara, Brooks, ed. 1983. *American Popular Entertainments*. New York: Performing Arts Journal Publications.

Nachmanovitch, Stephen. 1990. *Free Play*. New York: G. P. Putnam's Sons.

Nicoll, Allardyce. 1931. *Masks, Mimes, and Miracles*. New York: Harcourt Brace.

Petterson, Peter. 1864. *Glimpses of Real Life as Seen in the Theatrical World and in Bohemia*. Edinburgh, Scotland: William Nimmo.

Rico, Diana. 1990. *Kovacsland*. New York: Harcourt Brace Jovanovich.

Rubin, Benny. 1972. *Come Backstage with Me. . . .* Bowling Green, OH: Bowling Green University Popular Press.

Rudlin, John. 1986. *Jacques Copeau*. Cambridge, England: Cambridge University Press.

———. 1994. *Commedia dell'Arte: An Actor's Handbook*. London: Routledge.

Seldes, Gilbert. 1924. *The Seven Lively Arts*. New York: Sagamore Press.

Sennett, Mack. 1975. *King of Comedy*. New York: Pinnacle Books.

Spolin, Viola. 1963. *Improvisation for the Theater*. Chicago: Northwestern University Press.

Staveacre, Tony. 1987. *Slapstick*. London: August Robertson.

Stein, Charles. 1984. *American Vaudeville as Seen by Its Contemporaries*. New York: Alfred A. Knopf.

Sturges, Preston. 1990. *Preston Sturges*. New York: Simon & Schuster.

Sweet, Jeffrey. 1978. *Something Wonderful Right Away*. New York: Avon Books.

Toole-Stott, Raymond. 1964. *Circus and Allied Arts: A World Bibliography*. New York: Harper and Sons.

Towson, John. 1976. *Clowns*. New York: Hawthorn Books.